For Julia

Introduction

Four months ago, a producer at a well-known cable network wanted to speak with me regarding my story and how I built a business.

I was thrilled about the chance to talk and express myself. However, that quickly changed when he learned that my business was HR. He told me, "There is nothing sexy about HR."

That is complete nonsense.

HR is a wonderful field. And yet I knew what he was saying; I know what everyone says. After all, I went into business knowing about the bad reputation of HR. This is one of the many reasons why I am writing this book. It is time we start revolutionizing what HR is and will be.

When I first started to write, I was going to title it as *The HR Revolution: Revolutionizing Human Resources*. But as I have continued to learn during the creation of this book, I knew what I needed to do and say.

Human Resources is a brilliant field filled with sexy opportunities, wonderful people, and beneficial programs that can truly help a company.

Getting My Start

Life has a way of surprising us. After four years of living in the city, I found myself pregnant with my daughter before I had finished college. This changed everything. My exciting future was put on hold. While thrilled to become a mother, it was frustrating because that was not what I had planned. I did not plan to have children until after I made a career for myself.

It seemed that God had different plans for me.

Because I needed somewhere to go once my daughter was born, I moved back to my small town to be with my family. That provided me with the security I needed at that point in time, even if it was not what I had wanted. Part of me worried that I might never work in a professional field and would spend the rest of my life struggling. I loved my daughter and I wanted to do my best for her. Once situated, I started looking for work.

Our local prison was hiring in their business office because they needed a floater who could handle a variety of tasks for several of their departments. I was soon hired and placed temporarily wherever they needed work handled.

This included the Human Resources department.

It seemed like a simple role at the time, but it was quick to redirect me on a path that I had not even known existed. This was not a career that I went out looking for. My degree had been focused on Interior Design. I liked to visualize space and enjoyed creating something out of nothing. It seemed fun, not overly complicated, and exciting.

HR was something that chose me.

It was a role I had not expected to discover or enjoy and could not have foreseen its lasting effects. I accepted a permanent role in HR and knew that this was where I was meant to be. Everything fell into focus.

Once I entered the world of HR, there would be no leaving. I have dedicated my career to HR where I have had the opportunity to help countless businesses improve their processes and their teams.

My experiences have shown me how vital HR is to a company's development and growth. In seeing the need for progress in companies around the world, I have decided to share my knowledge within this book.

Moving Forward

Most HR books still address department problems in the old-fashioned way through strict processes with a technical perspective. From building materials for teams and learning to handle conflict, what the HR teams really need is more time and focus spent on learning how to bring humanity back into their department and organization as well as becoming more of vital business partner.

In this book, I share with you my past experiences, the lessons I have learned, and how to mend HR relationships within the workplace. I also share ways that leaders in an organization can build bridges with HR to have a more cohesive workplace. These chapters detail practices, attitudes, and behaviors exemplified in HR and leadership. It is important that errors of the past are discussed, analyzed, and studied to see how we can do better.

I believe that any professional can start opening the doors for permanent workplace change. We have a responsibility to the future to create updated ideas and lasting solutions. This book will address all these topics and more.

This journey through the world of Human Resources has not been easy for me and I do not expect it has been a breeze for anyone else. There were several times where I seriously considered stepping down and finding another career. After an atrocious experience early in my career, I spent several months reevaluating and questioning if this was the right path for me.

After much thought and many sleepless nights over my struggles, I knew that those past experiences could not be allowed to happen again to me or anyone else. I was smart enough to know that if this was happening in one organization, it must be happening within other organizations as well.

So, I decided that I was going to gain experience, study the old and revised strategies, and change the HR experience.

To create change, we must first change ourselves.

For myself, the first thing I needed to do was decide on the type of professional I wanted to become. Not just anyone could fix HR and start a revolution. All I knew at first was the type of HR manager that I definitely did not want to become. I did not want to be a scapegoat or someone who would let others walk over them.

That was a start! But there was more for me to do. I was not satisfied with staying the person who I already was; I wanted to be more. Looking at other professionals who I admired, I began to consider what to do. I needed to be educated, passionate, and focused.

I sought to combine all the great ideas and processes while removing the outdated systems and the dehumanizing aspects that still thrive in most organizations. I decided to pave my own way and help companies create the ideal HR.

It is a revolution, not an office lunch.

This book exists--so that we can go beyond the impossible ideals and build something that will last. Hopefully, it will outlast us while ensuring a future with a healthy system for all the professionals that are to come in the future.

At the end of every chapter, there are suggestions

on the next move you can make to get a little closer to establishing the ideal HR in your company. It is time to stop keeping this department out of necessity and to breathe some life into it, to go beyond the routines and norm.

HR has pretended to be neutral long enough.

When HR prioritizes employees based on their status and nothing more, there will always be complications. People become lost in the shuffle, valuable team members realize no one is helping them, and they tuck the real problems away to deal with another time. It is easier to focus on following the same procedures over and over rather than considering that each new situation may require another strategy.

There is something missing in all of this.

We need color where neutrality has lived. This is the skill of applying key principles to complicated situations and the ability to differentiate between patterns and people, which is better known as the *human touch*.

I want Human Resources representatives to understand that they are part of leadership and the discussions in this book about leadership are about them as well.

Nicole Anderson

Forward Motions

Words are filled with potential and power, which is why I have taken the liberty to highlight a few terms that will be used frequently in the following chapters. Everything we say and write matters. It is even more important in the role of HR to show clarity and exactness with our language to keep from causing confusion and hindering progress.

Humanity

> noun: human beings collectively; the quality of being humane

"Humanity is being able to find and develop the core connection that we all share."

In order to establish working relationships in the professional workspace, we must use our humanity to connect with one another. We need to face our differences and find a way to bond through our similarities. Though there may be incidents and problems during our careers, we need to confront these issues and use our humanity to communicate. We consider feelings and experiences when we use our humanity to ensure proper judgment, working conditions, and potential leadership decisions.

Emotional Intelligence

> noun: the capacity to be aware of, control, and express one's emotions, and to handle interpersonal relationships judiciously and emphatically.

"Emotional Intelligence is recognizing emotions and understanding complicated feelings."

Though often understated, emotional intelligence is the most important soft skill (something we will discuss in later chapters) that can be brought into an office due to the ability to better understand and connect with others. This means that an emotionally intelligent person will know both what is being spoken and what is being understood between the lines. An emotionally intelligent person can also be valuable in all roles because they can grasp complicated situations, understand what their team needs, and have better control over their own emotions to avoid potential arguments and embarrassment. Emotionally intelligent people use their empathy to connect with people and can help individuals become good leaders.

Empathy

> noun: the ability to understand and share the feelings of another.

"Empathy is the ability to understand why others feel the way they do."

Empathy allows leaders like yourself to use their soft skills, such as humanity and compassion, to relate to a given issue at hand. You must listen and learn. This provides you the ability to create solutions to problems you would not have been able to see if one of those traits were missing. By sharing empathy, you can build helpful bridges. Solutions created with empathy build a trusting relationship between employees and their employers.

Compassion

noun: sympathetic pity and concern for the sufferings or misfortunes of others.

"Compassion is the expression of sharing our spirit and soul with someone else."

The desire to serve and support others no matter their issues is to have compassion, whether in the workplace or elsewhere. Ego and control tend to run the workplace. More often than not, employees turn their heads away instead of putting their compassion and kindness to use for fear of being weak and having it used against them. Leaders who lack compassion tend to express their pride rather than nurture or express personal support. Every person in the workplace, such as yourself, should bring compassion to the office in order to be kind, efficient, and a team player.

HR is *Sexy*

These are just a few of the useful terms that we will be discussing in this book. Since you picked up this book, I know you are looking to change your workplace. Keep these words in consideration while you are reading and see how they relate to you as a professional.

I will illustrate my points throughout the following chapters and look forward to sharing my knowledge with you. Let us revolutionize HR and show how sexy it really is. I am eager for you to join us and see how we can change this department with its approach so that we can truly help every employee.

Part 1

Human Resources and Leadership

Chapter One

Taylor had just been hired into a junior role after college. Thrilled to be part of a great organization, Taylor worked hard over long hours and weekend shifts to provide good work. Everything was going well until a new manager was assigned to Taylor.

"I am switching to the tech department, and so there is someone else coming in to take my place," said his first boss. "Nothing should change for you. All that is different is you will have a different boss."

But having a different boss completely changed everything. Instead of an open-minded and energetic leader like Taylor had before, the new manager was old-fashioned who did not like to be bothered unless it was an emergency and never gave Taylor clear answers.

"What did you mean about this report?" Taylor tried asking his new leader about the new project he had been given. "I am not sure what you are saying in your last email and could use some guidance."

"Just read the paper again. You will get it," his leader said and waved him off.

Though Taylor tried to adjust and work with the new manager, Taylor's work began to suffer. So, Taylor went to the HR department to ask for help. Conversations went on for days as they tried to find a solution together.

"I want to be here," Taylor explained. "But my leader does not listen to me when I tell him I struggle to meet his constantly changing deadlines and I cannot get my work done if he does not explain what he wants. I tried to send him the project overview and he said I had it all wrong. But he just told me we needed a new banner for the company website and nothing more."

"Let me try talking to your leader," the HR representative decided. "Then I will come back to you."

Taylor hoped that the extra support would help the situation. He just needed someone who would listen and talk with him. He had questions and could not work if he did not understand what his boss was saying. Maybe HR could help him to find a solution.

However, once HR did talk with his boss, they decided between the two of them that Taylor was no longer a good fit at the company.

Though Taylor's work had been exemplary in the beginning, standards and expectations were no longer being met to ensure workplace success. Though Taylor had simply wanted help to find a solution to work better at the company, this situation ended with an unnecessary and unexpected termination.

Human Resources must maintain a balance that can, at times, feel impossible. It is much easier most of the time to give in and let a few responsibilities slide off their plate. They assure themselves and everyone else around them that they will tend to the problem eventually.

However, this attitude and loose structure cannot be permitted to continue.

Every job requires our focus to handle several matters of business at a time. We need to multitask when we are in a meeting to take notes, respect everyone in the room, and grasp the ideas being discussed. If we are capable of doing that, then it is also possible for HR representatives to balance their focus on the company, leadership, and their employees at the same time.

When this capability is ignored, someone invariably ends up hurt. A project can suffer, a team member may leave, and goals may be missed. This is clear in the story mentioned above with Taylor who was thriving up until new management arrived and made the workspace unnecessarily complicated.

While situations you experience in your own workplace may only carry elements of this story, it is important to take note of other resolutions that could have been created.

A lot could have gone differently to create a more open and honest space within that company. It is within the responsibilities of HR to serve every team member at their company, to create a safe workspace and to support those around them.

In the presented situation above, HR stopped listening to Taylor and catered to the leader instead. HR was inches away from seeing the problem at the heart of the situation, and yet still missed it. Their drastic consequences impacted everyone. Taylor lost a job that had started out very promising, the manager was left without that set of hands to manage their project load, and HR needed to start recruiting to fill the now empty role. Their final decision ended up costing the company money and time in the long run because of their short-sightedness.

There is no denying that relationships at the office can quickly become convoluted with restrictive guidelines, unfriendly attitudes, and other variables. People are not always easy to work with or to understand. However, that is not a justifiable reason to ignore the employee and the problem presented. While it may be a struggle to work with different personalities, HR chose to erase the problem without really fixing it. Thus, they lost the opportunity to find a proper solution.

This was a perfect example of HR in today's workplace. The department today either caters greatly to leadership or to employees. There seems to be no in-between. No gray areas and no balance. HR as we know it has struggled to balance its responsibilities in the workplace.

HR serves everyone in their company, not just the high-ranking figures.

I have seen this principle ignored time and time again.

Unfortunately, this is not a rare situation. That is why I am here: to remind you that it is possible to break from the norm and establish a better program and team that will benefit everyone within the company.

HR is currently encumbered with errors, old systems, and faulty procedures that do nothing to help the employees who could be struggling in a myriad of situations. Programs and systems have a way of being impersonal even though they are created by people. When something is made to last, creators tend to take emotion out of the equation. While this is done with good intentions, a system made for *people* needs to be better centered on ensuring a *personal* touch. The need for a streamlined system often can wrongly imply to others that a rigid structure is the only option without flexibility. It means rules are set up without consideration of exceptions or extended circumstances.

Because of this, HR can appear so regimented that it does not have space for compassion, humanity, or empathy.

This was one of the problems that I continuously experienced whether or not I was part of HR at the time. There were approaches and systems put into place that were doing more harm than good. A lot of the impactful efforts I have faced in my HR roles had strict procedures and red tape that were not doing anyone any good. We get so caught up in the need for compliance that we will throw out anything that does not fit.

Including employees.

It is only when a company, HR included, establishes a set of standards that defines their purpose and their work ethic so they can use that to fix the lackluster programs hurting their people.

A company needs a strong foundation in order to continue building and growing with its goal in mind.

Although a business is fluid and can relocate to any location, it can be similar to a building. A business needs a strong foundation if it is to withstand the test of time. When a business has that strong foundation, it means that everyone is working in the same direction because they understand the central goals as well as the roles that each person plays. This benefits the company as well as the clients.

Foundations

You may think that your company is headed in the right direction because there is a mission statement created and publicly shared on your website. However, more work is required than a string of words on the internet. A foundation means there is a firm understanding by everyone regarding the mission, vision, and core values.

This is something that must be decided upon when the company is established, and it should be frequently updated to align with the direction the company is moving in. Missions, visions, and core values need to then be shared with all employees, especially during the onboarding process.

Sharing the obvious ensures there is no miscommunication.

Mistakes can cost money, time, and jobs. We should always prepare our team members for success. This can occasionally mean doing some over-explaining to ensure everyone is on the same page. When you tell your coworkers that part of the company's foundation is communication, let them know what this means in the office.

- **Does this imply that everyone always needs to have their phones to be reached easily?**
- **How much can projects be openly discussed with different teams?**

- **Should people work through the ladder of connections or speak to the direct party?**
- **Is there an open-door policy for everyone in the company?**

As mentioned after the introduction, words can mean many things to different people. To explain your company's foundation without clarity is like a safe without the code. Make sure you are setting everyone up for success by teaching them about the foundations of the company.

When everyone is moving in the same direction, everyone wins. The role of HR is to bring employees together to fulfill the mission of the company, guiding the vision, and upholding the core values.

In fact, if done correctly with the right systems and strategies, it may appear that there is nothing more for HR to do.

Once management is functioning properly and employees are focused on their work with compliance made easy, we may ask ourselves, *is HR still necessary?*

Human Resources can be compared to jobs in the medical field by way of purpose: we want to help our people so well that they do not need us. The ability to be worked out of a job is the dream. That means we have achieved our goal. If our teams are so well communicative and operating that there is nothing more we can do to support them, then we will happily move on.

Be okay with losing your job for doing the right thing.

That is a motto that I have lived with for over ten years now. I use that for myself as well as others as a reminder that no job is forever and our career trajectory is never straight. This way I am always focused on my personal growth, and it is a reminder for me to stay humble.

It is also important to note that it can and will take a long time, with a mountain of difficult work, to reach the point of not needing that HR support. Especially since there is a lot more to our teams than simply healing riffs in misunderstandings and enforcing company policy.

Hopefully, such concerns will be addressed well through time, but there are plenty of responsibilities for the HR office to still manage. Besides the company activities and hiring process, there is learning and development and compliance that we are certain will never go away.

Due to HR's unique position in the workplace, we are both prepared and qualified to handle all the above-mentioned responsibilities. Professionals like myself diversify our skill sets to manage nearly every problem that comes through a company's door. With education and passion to support employee management, HR is specifically qualified to help each company to adapt and grow.

HR is *Sexy*

There is a foundation that was set up for HR as well.

It was an effort created to help employees find work satisfaction and to appease management with the tasks they had no time to address. The product of the human relations movement evolving in the 20th century, the updated HR was there to manage transaction work regarding payroll and benefits. These efforts continued to grow and the roles for various jobs have become hyper-focused. This means more work needs to be done by specialized employees regarding labor relations, talent management, company mergers, and more recently, diversity and inclusion.

More and more work has been loaded onto the plates of those within HR. And not only are there plenty of tasks to keep us busy on a regular basis, but the work is constantly changing. The way companies recruit new talent is more complex and busier than in the past. We balance risks, legal situations, and employee concerns.

To keep moving in the right direction along with the company, HR must remember the foundation on which this work was built. Our roles were formed to help the company succeed as well as employees. If we take any steps away from that, then we are no longer doing our job.

Our revolution is about helping us mend the HR infrastructure on a solid foundation that calls back to the original purpose and highlights how the workplace has changed since its inception.

The original foundation for HR is a good one, though it has been ignored and sidestepped for far too long. But it is not enough. We need to use those pieces and start to rebuild into something better. Establish that strong foundation within your company to ensure that everyone is guaranteed a fair chance to flourish.

Functional Pillars

With the groundwork laid out before you, now is the time to build the tenets of your organization. These pillars stand tall and help hold up the roof when things go sideways. When team members struggle and procedures fall apart, these pillars can keep you and your team secure.

Things go wrong in life and that means they will go wrong in your workplace as well. We should always be prepared. The smallest pebble can cause a grown man to stumble just like a missed signature on official paperwork or an ignored complaint by a team member can bring a company to its knees.

We do not want that to happen. So, let us make sure our foundations are solid and our pillars are strong.

Consider your compliance with policy and procedures. Whether they are new or old, and temporary or permanent. *But these cannot be outdated or misaligned.* They need to be purposeful and managed in an organized and appropriate manner that keeps them in sync with your HR foundation. These policies and procedures must correlate perfectly with your company's foundation to ensure a repeated pattern of success.

All company policies must align with its mission, vision, goals, and core values.

Every business is focused in one direction. Dedicated to a cause, service, or product, every business should know its direction and make sure every team member is aware of this. There cannot be room for any tasks or habits that ignore or bypass the foundation and pillars that have been specially constructed.

I have never seen any reason good enough to "ignore red tape" or "avoid clearance checks" when it would keep a company safe from legal or financial trouble.

When we decide that a contract needs to be signed without a legal review or that we can fire an employee without justifiable cause, we are putting the entire company at risk. Your foundation can prevent this. These pillars must be understood and demonstrated by everyone. This includes even the C-Suite, who often use their high position to skirt anything they might deem a minor inconvenience.

Setting standards means that everyone must be accountable to them. No one is free to ignore the hard work that everyone commits to once hired. The mission, vision, goals, and core values need to be aligned with everything that you and your teams are working to accomplish. Otherwise, there is confusion and room for mistakes.

For example, consider the dress code.

It used to be that every office required employees to wear suits, dresses, and polished shoes. Companies take pride in their work and their appearance, especially if they bring their clients into their office. However, as the workplace evolves, so do many policies. Now in many offices around the world, employees can wear jeans and sweatshirts.

I am not here to tell you it is wrong. I am here to ask you, does your dress code meet your core values?

Consider the situation if it is decided that one of your core values is creativity or innovation. These are important to your business and your employees should all emulate such characteristics. It is up to you to answer if it makes sense that your dress code is strict business attire or business casual.

These are not the only two options, but it is

important to consider that the guidelines, business practices, and work efforts provided to your employees work in tandem with the pillars you are establishing. When policy and procedure fail to align with your company's values, things are bound to go wrong. You send mixed messages. Your employees will see the gaps and you will begin to lose both their commitment and attention.

It is easy to get distracted, caught up in the big plans of management, and entangled in an old procedure or two that everyone still follows. No matter our position in the workplace, there will always be important tasks on our plates. But we cannot allow that to become an excuse for failing to implement and maintain a vital structure.

We must change the way we work from following outdated and impersonal manuals to bringing in that strong, personal foundation. This switch will help you and your team to build unity to help everyone focus on bringing their best work to the office.

Your HR Experience

Creating that foundation can sound like it is all about writing down ideas and rules that may never come into existence. And even if they do, there is a chance that no one may commit to them. Even a well-intentioned leader can talk about installing a new strategy of commitment and effort within the workplace only for it to quickly fail and be forgotten when the next big idea comes along.

The Human Touch

Human Resources, as it is currently, has lost that human touch. You can build and create all you want, but if you have not considered who your work is meant for, then you have accomplished nothing. One cannot put forth an effort to support humans without taking into account our nature and needs. This is what I discovered was missing and that we needed to bring it back to the office.

While I believe that people mean well, processes are sometimes organized to keep people from making better decisions.

The majority of employees do not set out to do a bad job, and most everyone in leadership would like to lead well, but people will always make mistakes. These mistakes cannot be ignored and left alone because they can damage an organization that will affect them in many ways, from their finances to their reputations. Ignorance is not an excuse to ignore the problems within a company. Instead, it breeds failures, unnecessary risks, and faulty services.

When we work with our employees to sort through their mistakes, we are helping. It will protect each of you along with the company.

People who mess up are still trying to do the right thing.

The desire of those in HR is to help a workplace work smoothly between all employees. We wish that everyone will be a good fit wherever they might end up, but we know that sometimes even after all we have done, there comes a time where we must consider opening the door to make room for a healthier situation.

Just because they did something wrong does not mean we shame or devalue them. We need to give them their dignity when we walk them out the door. These mistakes can be addressed in a tolerant manner without demoralizing or embarrassing employees of any level. This is a function of HR that is continuously tolerated when it should not be.

Whether our teams stay in place or are changed, HR has the responsibility to ensure that a continual level of respect for others is maintained at all times. Treating employees well during the bad times will create a long-lasting reputation with an environment of respect and integrity.

I have dealt with many HR departments that have no personality or flexibility. They have become the gray-walled, straight-faced, monotone department that everyone dislikes. Despite the commonality, that is not the employee experience we want to serve.

HR should be the place where all employees can turn to for guidance and support.

Employees deserve the right to have a department of professionals in their office with whom they can discuss complicated and personal matters that affect their employment. There needs to be a place where everyone feels comfortable enough to express their feelings and trust that what is said stays confidential. While one should not consider them to be therapists, they do fill a role of helping people sort through various problems whether it includes paperwork, professional relationships, or office responsibilities.

HR is a career that comes with hardships and excitement. This is not a role where you can just sit at your desk and leave the rest of the world behind you. HR should go above and beyond their office to build relationships with the other departments and leadership. The teams within a workplace need to be united, and it does HR no good to be seen as separate. They need to be viewed as a member of the team, not as an outsider.

HR Improvement

Such roles are vital in the workplace to ensure compliance, teamwork, and communication. Everyone besides HR, especially the leadership, needs a clear understanding of the role that HR plays in the workplace and the lasting (preferably positive) impact such employees can create.

Let us change the negative reputation that has chased HR since its beginnings. Every HR department has the golden opportunity to support everyone in their company. HR is one of the few positions with the ability to connect with every single person in the organization. It gives them a chance to improve and eliminate processes while making a lasting difference.

An HR department is responsible for the people in an organization engaged in the workplace experience.

In regard to all positions from entry-level to CEO, HR professionals are hired to ensure each recruited employee is given fair opportunities and is protected well enough so they can focus on their professional responsibilities. Due to their role in ensuring compliance and supporting personal concerns, HR can greatly impact the people in an organization. Not only can that impact be felt in an employee's time in the office, but throughout their life and career as well.

With the influence HR has in people's lives, every action and decision should be built upon dignity and integrity. HR has a responsibility to support the entire office, not just one group or another. We have to "right the wrongs" and do our best to make even the most difficult moments worth it for everyone involved. For our work to be effective, these values are vital to HR professionals like ourselves.

Human Resources is multifaceted in nature because it is an approach, a department, and a career all at once. It is an approach professionals use when keeping the best interests of the company in mind while handling sensitive issues that can affect the company's overall success.

HR is a department of representatives who support the company's legal concerns. They push the leadership's goals and values forward to fully develop employee engagement, support, and satisfaction.

It is my opinion that becoming a Human Resources representative is one of the best careers that a person can pursue.

Good Intentions

The origins of Human Resources were developed with good intentions. The role was created to make sure companies were complying with government rules and regulations. As worker rights continued to grow in popularity and importance, so did this role.

From where it started to where it is today, HR is now barely recognizable. The changes that affected the department were important, but they were also problematic. They did not develop at the same time as other areas in an organization.

Now, no one likes the one department meant to help everyone. Those good intentions became skewed and caused more lasting damage than temporary help. The wrong practices are formed, professionals are not well-versed in all their available options, and misunderstandings continue to abound.

HR has evolved into a strict compliance department. This is because we did not build a foundation of HR objectives with practices on how to improve the stream of paperwork and coworker incidents. That means no one is working in the same direction! So the work slows down, resulting in increased spending and wasted money.

Everything I share here comes from personal experience. After more than a decade of serving employees and employers alike, I have watched these behaviors and ideas hinder organization after organization.

If we are just moving problems from one place to another, we will keep tripping.

After its inception and desire to impact the

workplace, HR became a scapegoat for process managers because it was, and continues to be, easier to push off the hard conversations onto someone else. Leaders who are uncomfortable with discipline and terminations started using HR as a catch-all for all unwanted tasks regarding their people.

If a leader does not want to lecture or enforce their rules themselves, they will turn to HR. This way they remove themselves from the main source of contention or concern as though it will not affect them.

It is always easy to blame the middleman, after all.

HR quickly became the bad guy to both employees and leadership as they looked for someone else to handle the unpleasant obligations in the workplace.

> *"I am not sure I will say it right, so HR should probably be saying it."*
>
> *"I want to keep a good relationship with them and do not want to be the one to say this."*
>
> *"I would not know what to say. What if I upset them?"*

As the role of Human Resources grew more popular, the department quickly became known for policing employee behavior. This did not help their already tarnished image. A balance was necessary. HR employees felt that the only way for them to remain objective was to be standoffish and create distance between themselves and the rest of their company.

All of these things created HR's infamous reputation which has ultimately led to exhausted leadership and disgruntled employees. These types of results are deeply concerning, unnecessary, and harmful to any healthy working place.

Something must be changed.

Even if something is built with good intentions and established to help others, it still has the possibility of causing countless incidents. The framework for HR was good but the cornerstones used to build it have failed the people it was supposed to help.

Consider this: our current workforce contains six generations of workers, all with different mentalities, values, and work styles. Times have changed drastically just in the last couple of years as work phones and laptops have grown increasingly popular. As people, laws, and operations change, it begs an important question.

Why is HR not working differently too?

HR spends all its time making sure everyone simply follows the rules of the workplace, no matter how reasonable or unprofessional they might be. Most of the time they appear to prefer paperwork over actually helping anyone. Their time is spent commanding the troops, attending meetings, disciplining the masses, hosting a party here or there, and protecting the company from lawsuits.

I saw these problems arise repeatedly without them ever making sense. It did not make sense to negatively impact someone's life because of a simple dress code violation.

And I disliked how HR seemed to exist in its own little bubble. HR was the outsider that was only included through obligation instead of existing where it should– alongside the leadership team.

It is time that we moved beyond the status quo to provide real help to our workforce.

Beyond the Status Quo

With self-evaluation and reconsideration, we can instill new systems and strategies to support our organization. It will take time and effort to achieve this sort of change. Pride will have to be excused from the meetings and harmful attitudes must be improved if they wish to stay.

HR currently stands on a rocky foundation. It cannot last and will continue to fracture until it destroys everything in its wake. Already the outdated procedures are causing more than enough harm. We have seen what HR is and now we are beginning to open the doors to see what it can become.

HR is *Sexy*

The hard work comes next. Every system and strategy put in place within your company needs to be reviewed. Whether they are intentional or not, official or otherwise, recent or not, it is time to sit down and reconsider it within your organization.

You have to take a step back and let go of your personal preferences and preconceived notions to see how HR programs help or hinder others. Look at the hiring and retention rates, overall employee satisfaction, and how your company's services have been affected by your people. It is not easy, but it is the first step to moving forward.

As you complete this analysis, make sure that you and your people, especially those in HR and management, are prepared for what might come next. It is hard to hear when someone says you are wrong, and it is even harder to change your behavior.

Review our "Forward Motions" and when you are ready, continue reading to see how you can revolutionize your organization's HR department into something greater than it currently is.

Forward Motions

The first step is the most important one. After that, everything gets a little easier. So I invite you to start now with these steps as you work through this book. If that means you take days or weeks to finish reading, then that is perfectly fine. Refer to these steps as often as necessary to keep you moving in the right direction.

Step One: Decide What HR Means To You

Make a list of your current beliefs and opinions that you see in HR today

Whether it is five items or five pages, start thinking. You have read this first chapter and know what the world of HR is like at the moment. Do you approve of it? Consider its benefits and inconveniences, the problems you face daily, and what it will be like in the long run if nothing changes. While you are at it, decide if that is how you think it should be or if a change is necessary. Be honest with yourself. If you are a rigid HR professional who only sees your department in black and white, consider why that is the case. What would it take to open your mind to view things differently?

Step Two: Decide What HR Should Be

Write about what you believe the ideal HR looks like and functions.

After seeing the HR world as it currently is, define those outdated systems and misguided procedures that you see. When you put your thoughts on a page, they will become more clear. Write down how HR can be improved. Imagine that you could make immediate changes to the workflow process and compliance issues to ensure that all employees at your company can work more sufficiently and happily. Write down how your ideal HR operates with attitudes, strategies, and cross-departmental obligations.

Step Three: Choose Your HR Values

Decide on five values that represent HR in your organization.

You need to pick the right players to build the perfect team for football. In the same manner, you need to pick the right values for your HR department. These values need to be reflected in the effort that the team gives, and it needs to align with the leaders and their values. When your team members think about HR, these are the values that should come to mind.

We start easy here with simple tasks. Write these down and do not just keep them in your head. This can be completed within an hour or maybe it will take more time for you to put in the brainpower to make up your mind. Do what works best for you in creating your lists.

Active effort and accountability will be necessary for what comes next. It should be clear to you by now that a revolution does not come easily, nor does it come overnight. Now it is time to come down from your corner office or your ivory tower. It is time for change. You need to be ready for what comes next.

Chapter Two

When I was working at a national law firm, I was on my way to a meeting in the corporate headquarters one day. We had just acquired another firm and needed to sort through compliance concerns. Upon passing by the main conference room, I noticed there was a gentleman in there who was sorting and opening the mail.

Not only was it strange to find someone sitting there alone, but it was confusing because we had an organized mailroom elsewhere.

"What is he doing?" I asked my coworker.

"Him?" my coworker asked me. I nodded and he explained. "That is the CEO of the company we just acquired. He will be staying on in his role."

That was not the answer that I had expected. My mouth dropped open with surprise. "Then why is he sorting through the mail? Surely he has something more important to do with his time."

"I already asked him this," my coworker said with a grin. "He said that it keeps him humble. Handling mail is the only task that his staff will allow him to handle aside from his regular duties because doing anything more will mess up their tasks and routines. He said that if he can relate to his employees in handling some menial tasks on his own, every now and then he is able to build the company together with them."

"Wow," I told him. "That is impressive. I do not know a lot of companies who have someone like him working there."

●

Everyone has their assigned responsibilities and duties within the office. Pay differences and titles should not imply someone's worth or importance. Every job is necessary for a company to thrive.

In my career, I have heard it said too often by the C-Suite and even middle management that they are not paid to do *that work* or that they are too busy to handle the job duties that they personally deem below their paygrade. This conversation is dangerous for many reasons. It creates a deliberate and negative divide in the workplace that can make employees feel as though they do not matter. If leadership is unable to relate to their employees, then they are unable to take care of the employee's needs, understand their intentions, and see their efforts.

You are not the bee's knees, you are not golden,

and you are not better than anyone else. No matter your role or your experience in the workplace, you have a responsibility to listen to those around you. The common belief is not true: *an old dog actually can learn new tricks.*

Saying something is one thing, but doing it is another. We need people like this CEO mentioned above to help show the way, reminding everyone that we are all here to be committed professionals working together toward one goal.

The higher you rise, the farther you can fall. We do not want that to happen to anyone. That is why we are talking about this now. Everyone should be set up for success. Just because you have reached a certain level of achievement does not mean you have learned everything that you will ever need to know. There are times in my day-to-day life when I make my way over to my employees to ask for their advice and get their guidance. Everyone should be willing and ready to do the same.

Professionals need to be coachable, open to change. Especially in their particular areas of expertise. This is inclusive of everyone but especially business owners and human resources. Their roles are focused on managing the security of the company and the safety of the employees. Industries are constantly evolving and that means we need to continue learning in any way that we can.

If you are not ready to consider that you could occasionally be wrong and require more learning, then you are not ready to be in one of these roles.

Letting your pride win in the moment means you lose in the long run.

Individuals who are not willing to admit that there are opportunities for improvement are effectively damaging the organization.

Acknowledging your weakness is not a crime and will not destroy you or your role. It is about understanding that these are opportunities, not risks, and these pain points of yours can be a strength that you add to the betterment of your organization if you are willing to give it a chance.

Taking on the occasional small task is a great way to remind yourself and others that every task is important, and everyone should be paid fairly. Like this CEO, taking a few minutes out of your busy schedule to support your team will remind you to be humble, actively engaged in the office, and to understand the impact that your decisions have on the workplace, and it will show that you care about your company's success.

It is time to let go of your stubbornness so that you can consider that you may be setting back the progress that you desire to bring about.

Facing Reality

Reality often feels unkind because it forces us to face the harsh truths that we have been ignoring for however long we have refused to face them. Being humble means that you remember where you have come from, how much hard work you had to invest to get where you are, and that you know your strengths and weaknesses.

It is so easy to get caught up in success that you may forget that you were once a mailroom clerk or cashier.

Acknowledge the problems you see. Then remind yourself that there is always something you can do to improve your circumstances. Find the hiccups, the clogged pipeline, and the outdated processes that stand in the way of progress. Only by being truthful about the situation can it be properly addressed and mended.

Learn from the CEO at the beginning of this chapter with his modest example. He stayed out of everyone's way while helping them out with a simple task.

Any arrogance and pride are not meant to be part of the work or the attitude you bring to the office. Will it separate you from your competition? Possibly. But I can also tell you that such actions play no role in advancing your organization and they will not inspire your employees to continue working with you.

Humility is necessary; I have had several opportunities to remind leaders with whom I have worked with about this important trait. I do this until it is ingrained in their minds and hearts that they cannot do everything on their own. Without their employees, they do not have a functioning organization.

Every employee is just as important as the next, no matter their role.

Sometimes facing reality means taking on more responsibility and sometimes it means acknowledging that you are not the only one working hard.

HR and management need employees in order to be able to do their job. You cannot provide support without having someone there to support and you cannot lead without having anyone to lead. Turning your time and attention over to your coworkers is vital for business.

Often the problems that a company faces are rooted within and not outside the organization. Because employees are critical in ensuring progress, it is critical to treat them well and set them up for success.

One of the best methods for you to do this is to create a workplace where you would want to work. Strive for those values we talked about in the first chapter, provide quality benefits to set them up for comfort, and establish a workplace where you have always wanted to work.

This can include a range of possibilities from recognition programs, reverse mentorship programs, or cross-training. It is important to create an environment where employees are comfortable, safe, and eager to work hard. It should be a place where we would want to be if roles were reversed.

If you could not readily switch roles with an entry-level employee with their current work offerings, then it is time to take a second look at how you are treating your teams.

The ideal workplace does not happen overnight. It takes time and commitment to ensure that employees are well taken care of within your organization. This work will require leaders to step out of their ivory towers to understand their workforce. While doing this, management and HR need to be equipped with the tools necessary to successfully execute their company's mission. This ensures employees have their needs met and are empowered to be successful.

It is easy to look back on our past work and say that it was not hard to achieve because we have forgotten the time, pain, and effort we put in to get to where we are today.

As you turn your time and attention to your struggling employees, spend some time reflecting on your professional pathway:

- **Think about those who bet on you and bet against you.**
- **Consider who was there to help you when you needed support.**
- **Review the skills you taught yourself and how long it took.**
- **Remember how upper-level professionals have treated you and vice versa.**

The more comfortable we are, the more we forget that others may not be as comfortable. We can forget what it feels like to be treated badly so much that we do not realize how poorly we are treating our employees.

Remind yourself how far you have come and show your employees the path that you have had to take to where you are now. Showing them that you were once in their shoes does not make you weak. Instead, it reveals the strength that you have gained along the way and makes you relatable.

We have this crazy misconception that showing the weaknesses or problems we have had in the past is too personal to share in the workplace. But there is no reason for it. Why is it unacceptable to relate to employees to share your understanding and concern?

Building relationships is an important soft skill and one of the best ways to achieve that ability is to be relatable. Such attitudes and actions reflect within leadership abilities and can even help propel your organization forward by creating a more motivated and confident staff.

Your versatile skills and experience enable you to create your best.

It can do the same for your employees when you connect with them. When you address reality, you are helping everyone in your organization.

No one expects you to be perfect. That is an impossible concept that no one can reach, so you are better off not wasting your time on this idea. Instead, you should accept your reality.

Find the mistakes in your career and learn from them. You can additionally help others to learn from your actions as well. An organization, no matter its size, still needs to work as a team. That means being able to trust each person in their position and accepting the reality around you.

From the Bottom Up

It is easier to point the finger than to look in the mirror. When it comes to addressing problems at work, we want to be able to brush them off without having to do anything and hope that someone else will come to clean up the mess.

While it would be nice if everyone could take care of themselves in a manner to make your life easier, that is not the case. Instead, as Gandhi said, we need to be able to focus on what we can personally do to instill positive change.

When leadership is told that they need to change their results and outcomes, they will do everything within their means to change everything and everyone but themselves. No one wants to hear that they are doing something wrong or that they are messing something up. It is not easy to say and it hurts to hear. Even when the truth does get shared, it is often said in a whisper, to only select individuals.

When you ask for something, be prepared for the answer.

I can point out many times in my career where HR representatives and leaders have asked questions and then received the answer only to be upset by it. They never actually wanted the truth. They wanted a version of the truth that aligned with their perspective. When we negate the perspective of employees, we disregard their truth. It makes them feel as though you do not care and there will be no change in the organization.

For example, the Employee Engagement Survey will reveal the truth. That infamous yearly or biannual survey that you pay thousands of dollars for so that your employees can honestly convey their feelings with you and the company. And do not let me forget their expression of disdain for HR. Allow me to save you thousands of dollars in your future by sharing the top three issues that employees discuss on these surveys.

1. **Pay**
2. **Benefits**
3. **Leadership**

Though you may be willing to pay for these surveys, how many changes have you followed through on making after seeing the results? Did you create focus groups? Action plans? Prepare follow-up meetings to review potential changes? Create employee committees?

I will go out on a limb here because the vast majority of companies act this way and say that you probably completed one or two follow-up action plans only for it to eventually fall apart because someone decided it was less important and others realized that the change would never happen.

The problem is that it is easy to fix pay and benefits, but it is not so easy to fix leadership. This is inclusive of HR. The reason here is that leadership never believes that they are the issue. Instead, they think they are the bee's knees!

Leadership professionals are necessary to the company, their skills are pivotal in the success of the organization. However, leaders who are only Process Leaders and not People Leaders as well can be a detriment to their organizations. Turn to Chapter Four for clarity regarding the requirements for a good leader. I often work on training such people in various skills, both hard and soft, while helping to identify ways to improve their current workflow for improved short-term and long-term results.

However, I frequently run into a situation where leaders are promoted into such positions because they have made great achievements in their main responsibilities, but this is done without any consideration of how good they might be with people.

It is vital that leaders can actually lead their people and not just order them around. When someone in a higher position sets a clear example, then their employees are twice as likely to work harder and do better.

Though it may be a hard conversation and require more humility than one might expect, it needs to happen for both the company and that leader. People want to be their best and perform their best.

It ultimately is the kindest thing for you to lay it all out for them and let them know, "Here is your issue: YOU."

Doing anything less would include lies and ultimately be a major disservice to your company.

When you are told that you need to change, understand that it is not a blame-game and it is not about making accusations. We are not our flaws or our mistakes. To fix a problem, we must go to the root of the source. It is there that we explore the nuances and consider our options. Together, we allow such leaders to delve deeper into the situation and then create ideas to own the growth process.

Once we address the source and change our ways together, then we are truly fixing an entire work culture that will affect teams in the long run, as well as overall company growth and employee satisfaction.

HR is necessary here as well to see the gaps and how to pinpoint with leadership what is going on. Experts like myself need to be supportive and ensure that the issues are not taken personally.

Consider the situation from a bird's eye view: when you look at the situation from a distanced perspective, removing yourself from the situation, then you can focus more easily on discovering the perfect solutions.

HR and leadership need to work together to

brainstorm solutions. Then it is up to HR to research best practices to determine the right strategy and to see if it has been done before. People are often surprised to see that they are not alone in facing their professional issues. Together, armed with ideas and research, leadership and HR should then solidify a plan of executing permanent solutions.

Professional Requirements and Expectations

Solutions help us move forward. When we accept our faults, learning from our mistakes and intending to do better the next time around, then we are headed in the right direction. Competition in a workplace is a complicated balance to maintain because it often causes more harm than good.

No matter how your people may be organized or divided in the workplace, everyone working at your company is on the same team. Everyone works together. There is the central goal of the company to create good products and services, to help clients, and become a leader within your industry. This means that no matter your status, pay, or differences, you are meant to work together for something greater.

The overall focus of your work is the same, and so are the standards for everyone employed at your company.

This includes everyone who has been with the

company the longest and those who have just been recruited. The same expectations are made for every employee, for them to work hard and accomplish the tasks that they are being paid to accomplish.

Make time to review the requirements of your jobs and update the new hire onboarding documents. There, you can usually find details of your company describing the sort of employee they need and not just a worker drone. We will discuss more about your hiring culture in a later chapter to help you learn how to best bring on and support your employees. When you look at your onboarding documents, you may find descriptions that often include variations of these terms:

- **Ability to thrive under pressure in a fast-paced environment while supporting coworkers and customers,**
- **Enjoys multitasking and is detail-oriented with every responsibility, and**
- **Proactive team player driven by engagement and is highly collaborative.**

There is a bigger need now more than ever before to find not just a competent worker, but to find someone who is capable of fitting within the company's culture and focusing on the end goal.

Companies want to find someone who is committed and driven to help them succeed. That desire is understandable, and the hiring process needs to be thoroughly reviewed on a regular basis to ensure that they are recruiting the right people.

However, these descriptions usually get tossed away once they are hired. New recruits will start out on their best behavior but, with time, may grow lax. When they are eventually given raises and even promoted into leadership, it is easy to think they have everything figured out and may be able to get away with unnecessarily strict or unprofessional behavior. This is not the case, and it never should be.

Your job title means people are watching you, not that you are better than them.

There are requirements for new hires at every company, and there are still requirements for those who have been in their role for a long time. Higher positions do not mean that management can be disrespectful or disregard their employees. Rather, it is a reference to responsibilities that are added to one's plate. Leaders need to have characteristics for both the people who follow them and those who work beneath them. Characteristics like humility and a good work ethic can make any employee become as good as a leader.

Other attributes are necessary and helpful as well for employees no matter their status or skillset. Having a balanced variety of attributes is how great leaders are made. Leaders need to use such soft skills to work well with their teams and HR needs to be able to develop a balance of continual growth for themselves and be prepared to help their employees.

Everyone from the mail clerk to the CEO is important. When you can understand this and share the best of yourself while in the office, you are setting yourself up for success. Requirements and expectations for your position should be reviewed regularly to make sure that you are doing everything in your power to fulfill your official duties.

HR Inclusion

Solutions take effort and growth takes time. Everyone in the office needs to continually be working to fulfill their responsibilities. Progress will come. Even when things are moving slow and mistakes continue to occur, know that you are working hard and can succeed.

The best way to help you during those difficult hiccups is to take the next step by including the HR department.

You have done this by bringing them in as part of the solution, but what about the next project? What about all the concerns you have had? If you want those problems to go away forever, you are going to need help, and HR is the best place to find that help. The HR department is meant to be equipped with people who care and are eager to streamline new strategies with positive long-term effects.

One solution will not be a permanent fix.

It takes continual effort to move forward. To walk, we have to keep putting one foot after another in front of us. Just because we know how to walk does not mean that the knowledge will take us very far.

That is where HR comes in. This team can make those solutions permanent and then create safeguards against such problems in the future. They can also continue to watch out for these concerns in case they rise again and need to be handled. If they do, then you are ready and you will not run into long-lasting problems.

Everyone in leadership needs to be inclusive of HR. By working together, you are showing how other teams and employees can learn to collaborate and achieve the goals set by the company. People in high positions need to be setting an example for their employees.

When you are promoted up a level in your company, it becomes a chance to be a good example of ethical hard work and determination. It is not a chance to try proving you are better than everyone.

At the end of the day, we are paid professionals

who go home to our personal lives. Our careers are opportunities to thrive and change the world around us. But if we carry ourselves in a way where we are acting like we are better than others, then we run the risk of inflicting damage in our own lives and those around us.

You are not the bee's knees, and that is okay.

You are still capable of achieving great things. In order to do that, it is important to be honest, adaptable, and empathetic. These are just a few of the skills that will help you become a trusting and caring leader in your workplace.

Forward Motions

Now that you have started your path to changing yourself and your workplace, it is time to consider your experience up to this period of time. We are constantly growing and one of the best ways to see how we can grow is to look back and study how we did that in the first place. This might not be fun, but it will be necessary for you and your growth. Take a deep breath, let go of your pride, and get to work.

Step One: Reflect On Your Mistakes

Review one of the last times you made an error and where you went wrong.

Think about your mistakes or write one down, it is up to you. You do not need to make a list of everything you have done wrong. Just choose one of the last occasions, one that is fresh in your mind, and replay the moment it happened. Then backtrack and see where you could have done something different. What can you learn from the outcome you caused? How else could you have responded? What can you do next time something like this happens?

Step Two: Review Your Responsibilities

Consider the requirements and expectations of your hired role.

If you have not reviewed your job description recently, now is the time to pull it out. If you do not have one, then ask your leader or HR representative. They should be able to help out. If these are not easily accessible, then search online for a job description of your role to see the soft and hard skills that you should have at this point in your career. What more can you be learning? How can you find an opportunity to put these skills to use or test new abilities?

Step Three: Discuss Accountability and Insights

Make a list of your current beliefs and opinions that you see in HR today.

This step requires you to connect with someone. Preferably this would be someone you work closely with so that they can better address any questions and provide clear insights to share with you in this conversation. Once you have completed steps one and two, talk about them so you have someone else's perspective. They may know of other mistakes you have made that you need to work on, and they can steer you in the right direction for any help you might need.

These steps are meant to help you get out of your head and face reality. There is so much happening in the world, in our personal lives, and in the professional landscape, that it is easy to put these matters to the side and promise ourselves we will attend to them later.

Now is the time for you to act. These steps can take one minute or more, depending on your preference and availability. It is like ripping off a band-aid to help yourself heal. When you do this, you will also be helping your coworkers by setting an example and showing you are committed to your growth and efforts. Acknowledge your mistakes, remind yourself that you are more than your bad moments, and find a way to be better next time.

Chapter Three

Maggie had worked at ABC company for over five years. In that time, she became a very well-respected professional within the marketing department by building countless relationships with her coworkers and leaders. She had put time, effort, and care into getting where she is in order to keep growing. When the marketing director role became available, Maggie jumped at the chance to apply. Her interview went well and soon she was promoted into the leadership role directly over her coworkers.

Everything started out well. But a few months into her new role, two of her employees came to her with a complaint.

It was about another employee who did not seem to be pulling their weight on the team project. Maggie knew the project was behind schedule and in learning it was that employee's fault, she quickly became frustrated with the situation.

They did not have time to wait for things to improve, Maggie decided to go confront that employee right away. Without giving them a chance to share their side of the story or explain the situation, she scolded that employee. Maggie loudly reprimanded the employee and swore in front of her entire department before leaving them at their desk.

Caught off guard and embarrassed, the employee took a complaint to HR to report the incident.

The situation continued to fall apart. HR offers a surface-level investigation and eventually clears Maggie because they had deadlines to maintain. Unsatisfied at the disrespect, the employee attempts to reach out to the CEO, Maggie's boss, for support. But their CEO was busy as well and only wanted the issue to go away. Too busy to keep track of this, the CEO forgot, and the employee struggled to keep working under Maggie.

Once friends, the relationship became badly strained. She continued to berate him when she wanted to and went on to give him a bad performance review. Even though it was Maggie that created the hostile environment, the blame went to him.

There are different styles of leadership that offer different viewpoints, strategies, and potential relationships. Some styles work better than others and some methods simply should not be used.

An example like this may appear extreme but is not at all uncommon. Leaders do not have the time to sit around and talk matters though frequently, meaning they need to rely on what their team members do and say. This inherently is not a problem. Leaders need to listen to their team members. However, taking the situation at face-value and refusing to take accountability for how your actions may affect people *is* a problem.

You can see here that Maggie did not bring any rationale to the situation.

Several small adjustments could have entirely changed the situation around. Instead of berating the employee in front of the entire team, Maggie could have pulled him into her office to talk through the concerns she might have about his performance.

By giving him a chance to talk, this would give the two of them a chance to meet on middle ground. He could take accountability for his actions that might have slowed their project down. If this had happened, she might have learned that he was dealing with complicated situations at home that were adding stress onto his place. She could show her support for him by connecting him with their Employee Assistance Program as well as HR to see about finding additional support and resources.

With a conversation like that, the two of them

could assess the situation to look for solutions and plan to regroup in a certain amount of time. That would allow both of them to focus on the work that needed to be done, take care of themselves, and support their team.

Employees want to do a good job. They just need to be given the means to do so.

Management requires leadership, something that typically does not come naturally. Instead, it comes through hard work, experience, mentorship, and dedication. There are too many people in power over others who do not understand the aggression and unhealthy mindset they are bringing to the office and instilling in their coworkers.

People like Maggie mean well, but do not take the valuable time to consider the situation and look for the ideal solution. But it is important that we do not allow ourselves to take the fast solution because that will only cause harm in the future.

Leadership

HR and leadership need to work closely together to ensure they are doing their best for the company. They have to trust one another and exemplify that to the other employees for them to know that they can do the same.

When your leadership knows that they can trust HR to support them, cohesion builds boundaries for employees. The example within Maggie's story points out the rash and dangerous behavior showing how she was not keeping her promise and trust in her team like HR assumed that she was.

It is important for people in every position to work together to stifle drama and conflict. Not by killing it, but by communicating and trusting one another. This will make the working environment more conducive to productivity.

Such messages need to stem from HR since they have specifically been trained on how to support employees in every position. *You cannot just hope for the best.* Rather, HR and leadership need to be on the same page when it comes to expectations and employee support. Trust is important and without it, leadership is immediately put at odds with HR and is left with several problems. With HR's expertise, leaders can learn to properly handle their teams.

In Maggie's story, neither HR nor the leader was correct in their decision-making process. The various teams lacked trust and it created an "Us vs Them" mentality. That way of thinking destroys trust and reliance, thus negatively impacting productivity. This shows that an organization's culture and capability are a direct result of the behavior exemplified in leadership.

While we could list the various styles of leadership, such leaders typically fall into one of two categories as either a *People Leader* or *Process Leader*.

One style may come more naturally, which is the one people are advised to work with for themselves because it is very difficult to change more and more of yourself.

All types of leadership have a direct impact on relationships, productivity, and the bottom line within the company. At the end of the day, you will find yourself in one of these categories. You may be a People Leader who is skilled at communicating with people to motivate them to reach goals or a Process Leader who is an expert at handling processes and overcoming operational hurdles.

People Leaders

A dedicated team player, a People Leader focuses their attention on their people more than anything else. These are the leaders who are able to motivate their employees to work at 100% capacity because of their energetic and charismatic way of leading. From their point of view, they are a football team who needs each other to get the job done. If one person does not do their job up to par, the People Leader will see how it impacts the entire team.

This leader focuses on ensuring their team is

equipped for their job to ensure cohesion because engagement is their top concern. This leader believes that if employees are happy, then the work will move along quickly.

I worked with a client who had a dedicated leader like this. This leader fought hard to bring his team together, and in doing so he showed that they could trust that he would take care of them. Such an effort can do a lot of good for the team just like it can also potentially cause issues. Because his focus was on his people, sometimes the process was ignored or bypassed. This meant that sometimes production failed, and deadlines were not met.

It is People Leaders who choose to sacrifice a task to make sure the team is on the same page, giving up the bottom line for their relationships. These people focus on creating employee engagement with honesty and integrity. They know dignity is important and prioritize that as a strength.

Humans tend to congregate with those who they are most similar to, and People Leaders often have a way of drawing even more people to them because of their ability to create a welcoming and appreciative environment. They listen and acknowledge their team members with a dedication to an atmosphere with coaching, positivity, and learning.

But no leadership style is wholly perfect.

The main weakness that these leaders face is their struggle to stick with rules, compliance, and processes that are necessary to their roles. They care less about paperwork and handle situations on the fly. They work smart and effectively but are most likely to run late with deadlines.

HR will often get involved because of their issues regarding performance. When their focus is not on making sure that their projects are moving along but are bouncing around from one person to another to deal with each situation themselves, their projects will suffer. Productivity does not happen until they think everyone is ready which can take a long time.

To succeed, People Leaders will greatly benefit from receiving training around time management, operation strategies, and basic business concepts.

Such training will show leaders how to view the business in a 360° perspective rather than honing on one aspect. They need to learn how to manage their time to manage the business because people are just one, albeit very important, aspect of the job.

These skills can help balance out those that they already have. One of the best ways for them to learn is through peer-to-peer guidance because their social skills enable them to work effectively with and learn from a partner. Other options include gatherings such as conferences, trainings, and other group events because these focus on personal engagement where they can collaborate and learn from others.

Besides performance concerns, People Leaders tend to be a dream for HR. They typically handle employee relations issues well and with ease, often carrying a very low turnover rate. Because of their focus on employee engagement, HR will not have to deal with a lot of personal issues or contention.

HR will still need to emphasize the bottom line in these situations. If they do not help these leaders with their teams, then there is a chance that deadlines will be routinely missed, and overall performance could falter.

Putting programs in place and guidelines that must be followed in accordance with their leadership styles can be a great turning point for People Leaders. These programs should be personalized and discussed between the leader and HR.

Process Leaders

A driven professional, Process Leaders prioritize the task at hand to meet deadlines, keep organized, and ensure complete efficiency. They create an environment focused on company goals and cost-effective solutions with little patience for repeated mistakes that interfere with the operations. They tend to be more competitive with an "Us vs Them" mentality and are not always looking to collaborate or provide second chances.

This leader focuses on how employee relations are an additional task that will not produce money. It is these people who will keep your bottom line intact because they will do whatever it takes to make ends meet on their projects. Not only are they passionate about their tasks, but they seek to create an environment that is focused on their work.

I worked with a firm that often exemplified hard work and made employees into leaders before they were prepared. One recently promoted leader had implemented processes that made their steps more effective within the department by cutting out extra time and expense. Well-trained in streamlined processes, she struggled to be an effective leader as her employees began to call her out for her lack of attention and support. Her response was to write people up and then gossip about it. While there, I was working on the leadership training program to quickly pinpoint the problems to rectify these issues. But one problem that Process Leaders can face is preferring their former strategies that can use more updates; in this scenario, she used the program for a short while before reverting to her former behavior.

Process Leaders can appear difficult to work with because they are not usually socially interactive.

When it comes to employee engagement, they struggle more than others.

It is easier for them to order work to be done than to be social and talk matters through. Because of the effort they put in to balance out their problems, they can experience burnout faster than other types of leaders.

When HR gets involved, it may be tricky. Process Leaders love HR because of their strict observance of structure, but HR often has a difficult time in helping them get engaged with their teams to balance attention on the work product and their people. While this leader can get just about anything done for their job, they do not often build up their employees.

The best way for HR to support Process Leaders is to provide coaching in areas of conflict management, social skills, and soft skills. Reviewing work and providing adequate feedback is a great way to communicate with them, and outside sources for ways to learn on their own; books, seminars, and podcasts can be very helpful.

HR needs to emphasize teamwork in situations with these leaders. If they cannot help them to learn how to work with people and how to communicate, then the teams are more likely to fall apart and not understand how they are meant to work together. By putting programs in place on how to connect and mentor their team members, Process Leaders are more likely to succeed and bring their people alongside them on the journey to success.

Such programs should be personalized and discussed between the leader and HR to create the necessary changes.

Human Resources Leadership

Leadership and HR are similar in many ways that half their work is to focus on the company with documents and products, while the other half is spent on working with people through mentorship, meetings, and strategy. Their goal is to help the company through relationships and guidance as part of their regular responsibilities. It is vital then that they are always working together to meet the bottom line and create cohesion in the workplace.

Everyone has a responsibility to do their best for themselves and each other.

HR needs to show leadership that they present solutions and options so that leaders can comfortably spearhead the inclusion of HR within their normal integrations. Strategies can be created but often will not be implemented well or for the long-term if established by a team that no one respects or sees as a part of the organization. By working together, HR and leadership can change that.

Once everyone is aligned, they can get down to business. HR can do their job and help leaders do the same, and vice versa. This sets an important example for everyone within their organization.

Engagement stemming from leadership downward can establish necessary innovation within a struggling organization. This means collaboration and communication that leads to constructive progress and agreements stemming from between management and their employees.

The key is *constructive* progress. No matter your role or leadership style, providing quality support can make all the difference. Often the position becomes, "You are in trouble" when, instead, it should be, "I understand something went wrong and I want to work with you to mend the situation." While some personalities may not always mix, we need to always give people an opportunity to succeed. That will reflect more on us when compared to any financial gain.

Leadership Support

Support for one another requires time and attention. You need to understand what works for you and does not work, as well as your strengths and weaknesses. The better you know yourself, the better off you are taking care of yourself and your team.

Professionals, especially leaders, need to understand the faults in their egos so they can move far away from them. One of the biggest problems that management may encounter is having employees beneath them who know more than they do. A good leader utilizes the skills of their team for better processes, teamwork, and production. People leave their jobs every day to escape selfish and unsupportive management. We do not want the same to happen in your organization.

In order to help employee retention as well as company growth, you need to support your teams with a balance with both of the above-mentioned leadership styles. When you do champion them, your actions help create an environment where employees feel valued and the bottom line will not be negatively affected.

Every style of leadership still requires that you care about the people who work on your team. When this is not done, it can ruin your professional reputation and your company in attempting to hire qualified employees in the future. The way you treat one another affects business in every form. As the world continues to grow more focused on social justice and personal value, companies have to become more and more cognizant of how they present themselves to the public. Many clients today are cutting ties with brands that do not respect the values they claim or treat their employees well.

There is one meeting I attended years ago that has always stuck with me. Leadership is meant to provide support no matter their situation, including a disciplinary meeting.

I was asked to join without having an awareness of the situation. There was no time provided to prepare as I took my seat at the table beside them. This happens to HR when they do not share a healthy relationship with the leadership team. It does not always matter how much training and preparation is put into a job. Incidents like this still happen too often and situations can escalate as this one did.

Immediately the conversation began with the leader sharing a claim made by another employee about the young woman seated before us. "They told me that you were getting up a lot from your desk," he said. "Sometimes four times an hour?"

An accusation like that told me all I needed to hear. This was not going to go well, and we were already off to an unprofessional start. Not only was he addressing a claim made by someone else without seeing for himself, but the claim was about an action that was not breaking any company rules.

No matter what accusation is thrown out, HR is trained to understand there are always two sides to a

HR is *Sexy*

story. I was glad to see that the employee then started to talk and explain herself.

"I know, but I–"

Except she was interrupted. This was another telltale sign of a power imbalance and unhealthy professional relationship.

Her leader went on to explain how her work production had gone down over the last three weeks. Using this reasoning, he said that her excessive use of breaks was unacceptable in the workplace and not permitted per company policy because it was affecting everyone around her.

Had this leader consulted me before this meeting, we would have handled the situation differently. The employee was deprived of dignity and respect in this situation.

Facing these accusations, the employee in question began to cry. She then managed to explain her situation. Just a few weeks ago she had dealt with a UTI. In correlation to her health problem, she discovered that she had miscarried. Everyone's personal life affects all they do, including their work. Her physical and emotional health was struggling so she explained that because of these issues, she needed to use the bathroom much more often than usual.

As one might imagine, the leader had *nothing* to say upon learning the truth.

This is a terrible situation that no one should have to find themselves in within three roles set in this scene. HR was not informed, the employee was struggling, and the leader arrived without all the facts needed to make his case. Because his focus was consumed with the idea of lost production, he was not ready to listen until he had put all of us into an uncomfortable situation. Though the leader had never had an issue with his employee before, he held onto the claim and used it to make everything worse.

Leaders and HR do not need to be informed on an employee's personal life. That is not their prerogative, and everyone is entitled to their privacy. But it is also impossible to leave our problems at the door when we reach the office. Every professional does their best not to let their personal life affect their work, but there are extreme circumstances that are the exception.

The story I shared is a prime example of when a Process Leader comes out in full force without consideration of the people on their team. It is important that work gets done, certainly, but not at the expense of your employee's mental health.

Leadership and Employees

In my experience working with leaders and understanding their workflows and personalities, I have continuously run into three situations that need to be addressed. HR must work with leadership to ensure that these contrary ways can be corrected permanently and improved for everyone's sake.

1. **Leaders ignore their responsibility.** Because they are busy and do not wish to deal with situations they cannot control or are not certain how to handle, they leave it to the side or attempt to hand off their problem to someone else. There was a retailer I worked with who had a particular employee who was toxic toward her coworkers and customers. She raised hell over the smallest inconvenience and constantly caused issues. But leadership was not as affected by this, so they did nothing. This lack of discipline and refusal to confront serious situations, as small as they might feel, will eventually cause serious issues. When you have employees leaving because of a coworker, in any position, then you have played a part in establishing a toxic environment that will only cause others harm.

2. **Leaders make the discipline about themselves.** In disciplinary meetings, there is a very low chance that the leader will acknowledge anything they could have done wrong. HR is supposed to be there as

an intermediary because leaders are not faultless, and they are not always aware of the damage they can cause with their words. Too often a conversation can damage the reputation of their department as well as the company. Every disciplinary conversation I attended while working at a major retailer was solely focused on the company's reputation which meant that customers were always right. Leaders would prioritize customers over employee claims; I would attend those meetings and feel attacked even though I was only there to support the employees. Leaders need to listen to their employees and do what is best to help their teams. When the employees are respected and listened to, they can and will do a better job for their leaders and their customers.

3. **Leaders act before they listen.** When problems arise, it is easy to accuse and attack instead of asking questions and listening. The focus on speed and productivity only causes quality standards to drop. One of the CEOs I worked with had just hired a new salesman with whom they were constantly amazed by, thinking that he could do everything. The other employees, however, knew otherwise. They saw his work and could see that he had

lied about his credentials, selling the CEO lies. But nothing happened until the sales team started closing on a large deal when this new salesman jumped in and caused some issues for the decision-maker. The client backed out. When the CEO learned of this, he scolded the team but praised the new employee for a minor sale. He would not listen to the sales team about why this had happened and chose instead to threaten jobs and punish his employees. An action like this can cause lasting damage for an entire department. To be a leader driven to effecting change and streamlining progress within a company, you have to listen to your employees.

Leaders are put in place to both support and guide progress. The big picture is the continued success of the company. But that cannot take place without the employees, which is why leaders have to set their egos aside. A position is relevant to their responsibilities and not someone's worth. One of these responsibilities is to guide and help their teams thrive.

There are exceptions, of course. There will be employees who are not cut out to be leaders and there are employees who will not be able to adjust under leadership. Not every situation will pan out perfectly. That is why HR exists to sort through these painful situations and help leadership decipher when it is time to let employees go.

Everyone deserves a fair chance to professionally succeed.

When you let people talk, learn, and work, you are opening doors for yourself as well as them. Giving professionals the opportunity to succeed and thrive in an honest community speaks more about the organization and its leadership than any benefits that could be provided.

Leadership has a lot of responsibility on their shoulders. It must be wielded properly for the sake of the company lest they cause further harm.

Mentorship

One of the best ways to support employees and leaders both is to provide mentorship whether it is within an organized program for the entire company or it is built for a few professionals to work together for their betterment.

Mentorships stem from one-on-one lessons with teachers and tutors to cultivate not just knowledge but personal growth within the mentees. Ancient Greek philosophers and America's founding fathers all had their mentors who educated them and guided them to a way of thinking that helped them become the leaders they were meant to be.

Throughout the business world, less than 40%

of professionals have actual mentors to help them. Variations of mentorship and supportive relationships in the professional world have always existed. They are born through networking, company projects, and budding friendships. I have seen a difference between organizations who promote these types of programs and those who blatantly dismiss them.

Building internal relationships, such as in mentorships, are one of the most neglected areas within a business. The focus is so much centered on churning out product that they bypass the understanding that relationships make everything smoother along the way. Excuses get made like:

> *"We cannot take time away from our desks."*
>
> *"The costs for this are too high."*
>
> *"I do not have time to sit around when I have more important things to do."*

When the company culture is focused solely on the bottom line, it is vital that programs like these are established to cultivate a space of learning and effort. This is more than just having a "second boss" with someone to whom another is held accountable to in their professional goals.

The cons are worth it in the long run. Over the last couple of years, there are mentorship programs in more than 70% of Fortune 500 companies. This is one of the reasons why they work well together in their teams and are able to continually succeed. Among the professionals within such supportive programs, 97% claim that these mentorships are valuable. The majority of young professionals say that mentorships would be vital to their growth; as companies grow too busy to pay attention to their employees, they are missing an opportunity that could drastically impact the business in a positive manner.

Nearly 90% of mentees walk away feeling more empowered and confident.

From the first day of the onboarding process, new employees need to be properly educated on the business and about their role. One of the best ways to do this would be with a helpful resource, such as a "work friend" or assigned mentor.

Right off the bat, you can help your new employees start cultivating a relationship with a coworker who advocates for them in the learning process and advocates for the company to the employee; that will establish commitment between both parties.

When someone new comes on board, they must be made to feel comfortable there so they are ready to focus and get to work. This will speed up the onboarding period and help them to learn faster. It helps everyone to be on the same page about the company and their roles, alleviating concerns over miscommunication and unmet expectations. Providing a personal touch to their training process can sometimes make all the difference.

Employees who are supported in the very beginning of their new roles are more likely to stay on longer with the company, improving overall retention. When given everything they need to perform the duties of their job in a place where they feel understood and respected, it decreases the rate of professionals leaving for another job. A company needs to show it is committed to an employee for that employee to commit to the company.

Loyalty is great, but what is better is when you have an entire team completely committed to a mission because of how much they respect and appreciate the people and brand for whom they work. Mentorship can help cultivate this because it connects different levels within teams.

From the C-Suite to entry-level employees, everyone should have access to a mentor.

Support Your Team

Without some sort of support, people have a tendency to flounder. This will happen within any given role. Even go-getters and independent workers need help along the way whether it is through guidance, compliance, or for another reason. Not only do professionals need someone available when they are ready for that help, but help may need to be given before they realize they need any aid.

Supporting your team can be seen in several different methods.

Consistency in your actions, decisions, and policies is one example. This helps your people to know what to expect from you at any given time. It helps your team to stop guessing daily what the workload and organization are going to look like. When you are consistent, your team will know they can trust you.

It shows who you are, what you are capable of, and helps others to know how to approach you. Leaders need to be more than a name and a face. Teams need to know what makes their leader the way that they are; with better communication and understanding, the more likely all of you will work in a cohesive and productive manner.

Leaders can also show their support for their team through their discipline strategies and how they engage everyone through innovation.

Improve your workplace and you improve the people working there.

It is helpful to guide the way and show your team how to tactfully communicate and manage new processes. Employees learn the skills necessary to respect and work alongside everyone this way, including working with those whom they may not agree with or particularly understand.

Your example will show them that they are capable of overcoming disagreements to focus on the bigger matters at hand. Leaders need to create an open and diverse workplace where all employees are eager to work and feel capable of doing a great job.

Additional tips to support your team includes:

- **Understand your staff.** Take the time to learn about their complexities, preferences, and how they work best. Discover each employee's skill sets and work together to learn how to make them stronger on the team.

- **Learn what they can offer.** Employees want to do a good job, so set them up for success. Through peer groups and employee engagement surveys, you can find out what your team knows and wants to be more engaged in.

- **Analyze your gathered data.** From your groups and surveys, create a strategy to implement your ideas and changes.

- **Build training programs.** Based on your results, create the programs that will benefit your teams the most. This can include online courses, instructor-led courses, inter-departmental training, and more.

- **Learn from the experts.** Work with your teams and leadership in being taught by the experts of the departments. They should support the cross-training strategies and will help equip other professionals with similar skills.

These are just a few of the helpful tips for leaders to begin training the mature workforce they are looking to establish. Sometimes we have to take matters into our own hands to help others learn. With these ideas set in place, you can have a workforce that is diverse and eager to help you build up your company as much as you.

Leadership Discipline

There is an unfortunately large portion of HR responsibility that is typically engaged in disciplinary action.

No one is perfect and mistakes happen. HR often gets involved to try and keep such a problem from happening again. In order to maintain a balance of structure, progress, and responsibility, you need to stick with values. Whether they are the set values of your company or your own, they are necessary to build your actions upon.

HR is *Sexy*

Especially when it comes to HR because of our middleman role. Our job is to support everyone in the company. We are in a position to affect someone's life for good or bad. Every person deserves the right to maintain their dignity whether they are being praised or punished within the workplace.

There will be times, whether it is decided by HR or leadership, where an employee is let go from their role. When they leave to walk out the door, do not shame them. Even if they did something wrong, it does not mean they should be treated less than anyone else.

Hurting people like that will end up hurting you, the company, and others. There are several risks involved with treating former employees badly. And I can tell you that it is never worth it.

It is part of my role occasionally to handle terminations. This process is never easy, but I am relieved to know that I have never had a single employee complain that I embarrassed them or handled the situation improperly. On a few occasions, I was even thanked for treating them so well with respect and dignity.

However, when I worked for a national law firm, there was a terrible event that has greatly impacted the way I manage people today.

The company chose to lay off seventy people the

week before Christmas. Leadership did this in order to show a profit at the end of the year after acquiring two firms and had even held a town hall several weeks in advance stating they would have no layoffs. But this was done anyway. This was out of my control and has left a bad taste in my mouth ever since.

Every action will experience consequences. During the following year, while we were attempting to fill some positions, we had such a bad reputation that we could not pay people enough to work for us. The public knew what we had done, and they did not want to be part of something like what they had done.

People are watching our actions no matter our roles and responsibilities. One must have integrity in the workplace to help others maintain their dignity. You cannot run a business if you do not have employees who help you do the work. And when you bring values into the mix, you are more likely to find efficiency, commitment, and dedication.

Leadership Values

It is easy in one moment to think that in a certain situation, you would react in a certain way. However, that is not always the case. Especially when you are not aligned with a set of values, you stand on rockier ground. By having values set up for your company to focus on as well as personal values to stick to, you are

HR is *Sexy*

giving yourself a chance to succeed as well as your employees.

Dignity and integrity are core values that I believe are necessary within every workplace.

In regard to dignity, it means to honor and respect someone regardless of the situation they may be in at any given moment. This promotes self-worth in everyone. It is a reminder that we are not our flaws. If everyone knew the mistakes you once made, would people still have the same view of your character? I consider this every time I am in a situation where I must investigate or terminate someone. Even if someone is a repeat offender in their mistakes, they still deserve to be treated like a person. If their personal lives are falling apart, they do not deserve to be treated any less human.

Because of this, I strive to ensure that someone is treated well going out the door as they are when they come in for the first time. That is regardless of any mistake they might make. Though it may be difficult at various points, I remember to give others dignity because embarrassing, demeaning, or berating will not fix the situation; that only makes everyone feel worse.

Integrity is very much like dignity in that it goes beyond our natural instincts to be better and help ourselves so we can help others. Dignity is much more personal compared to integrity as it focuses on giving what we have instead of using what we have. These values need to be shown with the company culture.

To support the business, they must be built into a workplace through effort by the leadership team. They should also be found in the individuals that HR hires. The trick then becomes how to hire the right people. After all, you can give someone dignity but you cannot give or teach integrity.

These values may appear different to one another, but they belong together. Prioritized by the company, they can set the standard of how leadership reacts to them and how employees are helped during the hiring process. When you have a framework of values you want to stick with, then you will attract the right clients who come begging for an opportunity to work at your company.

By building these values into the company culture, you are setting the groundwork for your teams in the future. It then requires continual effort on part by everyone, especially leadership, to ensure that the values remain intact.

Once I worked for a flooring company where my role was situated directly beneath the Vice President of Human resources. This leader was the best mentor I had ever had up to that point in my career. He taught me that emotion in HR is necessary so you can be empathetic towards others and to always remember their situation is relevant to them, not me. I will not always understand what they are experiencing or going through.

One day, our CEO walked through the office and fired ten people because he had decided to change product direction. My leader stood up fearlessly to make sure the CEO knew that his actions were wrong.

People should never be treated as though they are disposable, and it takes time to put plans into place. My leader taught me about courage and how a CEO is the same as any of us.

We should never be afraid of losing our jobs for the right reasons. Both leadership and HR have a responsibility to each other, the company, and their coworkers to stand up for what is right. It does not matter who is making the mistake because this act is about putting values before profit. Everyone should hold onto and use their dignity in their given position for their personal edification as well as the company's benefit.

Forward Motions

There are various leadership styles that have proven effective in business, politics, and other parties around the world. The two things every good leader sticks to are their dignity and their commitment to achieving their goals. Of course, this can only happen deliberately. By following these steps below, you have a chance to reflect on your current strategy for your leadership and how you can improve yourself.

Step One: Identify Your Leadership Style

Narrow down your leadership style while reflecting on your past work experience.

Based on your personal experiences and values you should be able to tell just what type of leader you tend to be in the office. Even if you do not have a role where you are directly above someone else, you can see in the way you engage with other employees what your style is like. As you reflect, take into consideration how this style has helped you and how it may have also hindered you during various occasions.

Step Two: Discover Leadership Compatibility

Reflect on the leaders you have admired and worked well with in the past.

You will have worked with other team members in leadership roles whether they are directly above you or not. Take this chance to review those you have worked well with in the past and why that might be. Note the values they succeed with and how you can do the same. When you learn to understand someone else, you can begin understanding yourself better as well, both your experiences and your potential.

Step Three: Review Leadership Styles

Make a list of your heroes with their leadership styles and values.

Similar to the task above, you are casting a wider net now. Instead of someone you have directly worked with, focus on another figure who has impressed you with their journey of hard work to success. Study what you know about them to better grasp their leadership style. As you do, see how well they match the values you subscribe to. Then ask yourself if those are the values you want to use in your life and how you can make that happen.

We are masters of our fate and do not succeed or fail by accident. Everything we do needs to have direction. By reviewing our values, we may find that we need to work harder on one or potentially choose another one to focus on. These will help us refine our skills and build healthy working relationships.

There may be people who appear to be natural leaders in the way they talk or walk. But as you study them, you will find that they subscribe to other values that have helped them make it this far. We need to be deliberate in our actions around others as well as ourselves. It is only then can we be our best and do our best.

Chapter Four

While I was working for a national law firm on their leadership team, we were given a budget for employee engagement. It was decided to be 15 dollars per employee per month. Through brainstorming and several meetings, our leadership team decided on a strategy that would allow us to plan ahead and benefit everyone: the budget would be used collectively.

Instead of small events and activities that required maneuvering time away from our desks, we elected to host a few big events throughout the year.

Our employees loved this.

These opportunities, though only a few times a year, allowed everyone time to step away from their stressful lives to enjoy each other's company in a non-work event. We brought everyone together for food, music, games, prizes, and just plain fun.

People would talk about these parties throughout the year. It gave them something to look forward to and effectively built a close-knit community in the office. I thought it worked out great to support their hard work and provide a fun reward.

And even though I, with many others, could see the difference in giving these opportunities to our employees, it did not always please everyone.

"Why are we doing this?" Someone would invariably ask at each leadership meeting. The complaints would continue. "We do not need to go out of our way for this. Everyone is too busy. Besides, we are wasting money on these people. Isn't their paycheck enough?"

●

The last question is an exact phrase I have heard repeatedly throughout my career. There are always professionals and leaders who want to know why a paycheck is not enough at the end of the day for people to work hard, do their job, and come back the next day.

A career, any job, will typically appear as a basic transaction. One person works hard to help someone make a profit or benefit their life. In return, the other party pays them for their time and effort. Should it not be that simple? Why should we convolute it with additional bells and whistles?

Especially when people fear those bells and whistles receive *too much* attention while there is work to be done. There are reasonable concerns about providing a lot of benefits and additional perks. Often that means you need to hire more people, talk with lawyers to make sure it will work out, and spend more money than you might have intended to return into the business. Leaders want to be able to focus on the end goal: making their business thrive. Workers come and go, so why should we worry about what a few of them want?

Unfortunately, it is this sort of mindset that will push people out the door.

There are several reasons why the benefits and perks within businesses continue to grow and evolve. Jobs just are not the same as what they used to be. There are differences that we need to take into account such as the generational difference, cultural considerations, and more. We will explore each of these options within this chapter to understand why this matters and how to make this work for you and your organization.

Generational Changes

The working world has continued to change and evolve throughout the years. The way our parents and grandparents worked is not the way we work anymore. Every generation brings something new and takes something away.

We have gone from the terrible practices of serfdom and slavery to where anyone can start a business. As laws were changing, everyone adapted to indentured servants with pay and housing for many years, sometimes a lifetime. Millions of people have suffered and died because someone else wanted to make more money. For a long time, it did not matter how old someone was while they worked or how closely someone unknowingly worked with dangerous chemicals and machinery that could kill them.

Labor laws came into place to ensure the possibility of protection and guaranteed pay of services rendered. That became enough for the working class at the time. The transaction was agreed upon and made. Businesses were in charge, so asking for too much could cost a person everything. People went to the factory or office to work and then they went home with a paycheck.

This worked well for the older generations like Baby Boomers or Generation X (Gen X).

It is understandable that they would assume that this would be enough for the following generations. Surely all they needed was the paycheck and everyone could continue to work as before, thriving and moving the economy along.

But it does not work like that.

One has to be able to see the entire picture and

not just from a glance that provides a limited view. There are extenuating factors that will play into any situation, especially one that encompasses the differences between generations.

As the world changes, so must we.

The idea that people come to work to make money, go home, and live their lives peaceably dates specifically back to the '40s and '50s. Employees were satisfied with a wage that paid the bills and put food on the table.

However, with the development of the modern workforce since that period, this idea has required modifications.

Our American middle class is shrinking. With the rising costs of college tuition, housing, and healthcare, having a disposable income is quickly fading away. The top one-percenters in the world are continually reaching new highs while over 10% fewer of the younger generation, otherwise known as Millennials, are middle class in comparison to Baby Boomers. When their growth is compared, even during a booming economy, the older generation wins with steadier incomes, more possibilities, and less concern over downward mobility.

This means there is less financial security for the

generations after the Baby Boomers. There is the risk that social security will not work in their favor when they are ready for retirement like the Baby Boomers, and pensions are rarely offered any longer.

Even as Millennials put in more time at the office, they are making less money.

The federal minimum wage has remained static while the cost of living is constantly rising for young professionals seeking to join the workforce. Without making a fair wage, professionals struggle in their home life and will essentially struggle in their work lives. It has since been proven that workers living in poverty, or close to it, are more inclined to face mental and emotional challenges while working and trying to stay afloat. A company cannot claim to treat its employees with dignity when they are not affording them a better situation in life.

These wages were sufficient for the older generations but many are not now.

It is not just about the financial concern, either. It is stemming from a generation that has had more opportunities and potential at their fingertips than most generations before them. When we are able to separate these generations and look at the big picture, we will find that we simply cannot treat everyone in the same way.

Nicole Anderson

Not Cogs, Just People

Currently, many mid- and entry-level professionals are rising from the younger generations. These individuals have grown up consistently experiencing instant gratification in all aspects of life; as a result, they expect the same experience at work. They want to be acknowledged for their services and treated with dignity and gratitude.

This desire cannot be ignored. It is less important to a business when their focus is on production but it may be necessary to ensure young professionals support said production. As hard as it may be for organizations to accept, the younger generations will make up a majority of the workforce in the next couple of years. We must be willing to find a middle ground between our needs and desires in order to work together.

Expectations need to be met from both sides to create the right solution.

To successfully retain employees, companies will need to offer just a bit more than they used to so they can cater to this new perspective. While this is not initially appealing for your organization, keep in mind that you need people to keep your business running.

Prioritizing your employees will create lasting benefits for you and your company.

If employees stay with the company longer, the financial burden of turnover can be shifted to strengthen programs that assist in attracting top talent. Commitment now comes at a higher price because of all that the workforce offers.

Overall, the younger generations believe there should be more provided at work than just a paycheck. There are a lot of jobs open that need to attract top talent. When people know their worth, they expect to be paid for it.

You should consider these questions:

- **Who keeps the business running?**
- **Can we bring in the same profits or higher without employees?**
- **Are they being paid adequately to justify never receiving appreciation?**

You will find that you do need your workforce and, most likely, you need to be doing something more to show them your appreciation.

As shared in my story above, I exemplified how small acts of kindness can go a long way and complimentary gestures can improve team effort and unity.

Sometimes spending a lot of money on a paycheck is not even what a person wants. Every generation values different things. In fact, when surveyed, 79% of employees have said that they would prefer better benefits and perks rather than a pay increase.

If a company cannot afford to highly or competitively compensate its employees, the best alternatives are appreciation and recognition. This can be as simple as celebrating their success with cards and swag or providing a team lunch on occasion. It takes very little money to put a smile on someone's face and thank them for doing a great job.

Many of the changes that employees want stem from how the professional world is changing.

The correlation is clear once you start to look for it. Visible on the world stage, the booming technology industry brought a more casual approach to the workplace. It revolutionized the world in terms of possibilities, products and services, and the employee work life.

Many such companies are now offering hefty packages of benefits inclusive of nap times, unlimited lunches, and jeans as the new business attire. Following suit, several other industries and companies have now adopted this casual, employee-centered approach to the workplace. With the job market booming, employers had to find creative ways to attract and retain top talent. This meant more and more employee benefits could and *needed* to be offered.

Picture two companies alongside their offerings to see this distinction:

- **Company A offers standard benefits of ten days paid vacation with employee-paid health insurance, 401(k), a livable wage, and a holiday party at the end of the year. This is acceptable, legal, and employees will survive on this offer.**
- **Company B offers a competitive wage with guaranteed annual bonuses and profit-sharing, plus three weeks paid vacation, employer-paid health insurance, three parties a year, and has just included a gift card incentive program to stand out and attract new employees. This is acceptable, legal, and employees will survive and thrive.**

The first company is giving their employees what they need to function in their roles and makes sure they are equipped to handle the job. None of this is wrong, but it may be seen as offering just the minimum whereas the latter, Company B, is going over and beyond in treating their employees with dignity and additional perks.

Many organizations like to say that they boast that their employees are like family. If this is how you do it, then take time to answer the following questions. How do you want to treat your family at the office? Doing a little bit to help them, or doing everything you can to help them? The happier an employee is in their office, the more likely they will stay.

When you reflect on your organization, consider all that is being done to help your coworkers no matter their situation in their personal lives.

Do they have families? Health problems? Children on the way? Are they happy with the benefits provided? Could they be happier, and thus more productive, with better or more benefits and perks?

Incentivizing Employees

Incentivizing employees is all about finding a balance between effort, profit, and expectations.

Alongside the essential benefits are incentives, perks, and prizes that are meant to encourage employees to work harder and do better. When we have something to look forward to, it helps spur us into action.

These types of bonuses are popular especially at call centers where the hours are long and the work often feels unrewarding. To help their people endure and move past the bad calls with occasionally unsatisfying effort, these companies will provide team-building activities, extra meals, and frequent prizes they can win.

More companies are beginning to participate in this type of employee engagement because it has been proven to work. Creating an incentive program, specifically structured with employee input, will have a positive impact on your company's goals, whether they are based on quantity or quality work.

It is also important to note that the long-term incentives have been proven to work twice as well when compared to short-term incentives.

I have seen it in my career repeatedly: the more that a team is shown their value and the more each employee feels they have something to work toward, the more they are going to give their job all their energy.

It is important that the leadership is shown this positive workflow with the support of HR. These teams need to work together to create the best working space for their employees. Even rewarding people before the task is finished can help prompt more effort.

As we balance out the responsibilities between leadership and HR, the question arrives about who should be the one providing these incentives?

The answer is both.

Incentives should be given equally from leadership and HR.

They should work together even if they are presented in a different manner. Ideally, each leader will provide incentives to their teams. They need to be able to show they are committed to, care about, and are aware of their team's hard work. HR should always empower leadership to take the initiative to reward their employees. By working together to find the right incentives and rewards, leadership and HR can be seen as "the good guys."

Incentives should be decided upon by the entire leadership team, in combination with HR, to ensure that they are fair and consistent while keeping the organization's mission and values prioritized.

HR's priorities should be focused on the macro level with the scheduled incentives gifts such as work anniversaries, birthdays, monthly cultural events, and so on. As for leadership, they should maintain the performance incentives, awards, and even daily incentives if desired, when it comes to their own teams.

Both departments need to be ready to work together and serve their teams. Not only will this build communication and fluidity between efforts, but it shows your coworkers how collaboration can and should be accomplished.

Working together effectively helps everyone achieve the company's goals. We cannot let ourselves assume we are too busy or distracted by more important matters. Those in higher positions with grand titles need to be seen setting an example for their people.

When promoted, it gives you a chance to set a good example of ethical hard work with a determination to succeed. This is just a reminder that it is not a chance to try and prove that you are better than everyone.

HR and leadership are the guides in making sure the company moves effectively. When they show they are willing to provide more than just a paycheck, it helps their employees know they are in good hands.

The Benefits of Benefits

The perks you provide your people show that you care and are committed to employee welfare and success. It also allows you to create teams of hard-working professionals and achieve your goals more quickly and efficiently. There are countless benefits that come when you give back to your employees. Studies are continuously finding more reasons for you to give those incentives to your teams.

As discussed above, providing incentives can help your team members stay committed to the brand and inspire them to stay longer. Whether they are financial, culture-related, or something else, there are a lot of opportunities for your company to exemplify the core values you preach.

People want to be where they are respected and cared for.

Having an open and friendly company culture can go a long way in supporting your teams. This helps them have a professional support base they can turn to when they are struggling.

When your people can turn inside the company for help and guidance instead of outside, you keep them close and have a lower risk of losing them. Ultimately, this supports employee retention and saves money in the long-term.

Another benefit could include potential tax breaks.

Already there are many companies who have learned that donating leftover food or offering gas reimbursements can earn them a break from government demands. Health insurance is inclusive as well. There are plenty of options that you could take advantage of that will go a long way in benefitting your team and people.

Take education, for example. There are programs now to support employees who desire to grow their skills. Whether it is college courses or certifications, tax breaks may be afforded to companies who are dedicated to helping further the education of their employees. *It shows that you are willing to invest in your employees.*

When they continue their education and are able to earn more certifications, this will open more doors for your company as well as ensure your teams are providing their best effort daily. They may feel indebted and thus inclined to stay with you longer, if not for their entire career.

When you treat your people well and provide great incentives, they are less likely to leave.

The benefits that come your way, whether through HR or leadership, are bound to exceed tenfold when your coworkers feel they are well-respected and no longer just a cog in the machine.

When asked, 60% of employees said having a benefits package is extremely or very important to ensuring commitment to their employer. Then there were nearly 40% of employees who say that improving their benefits package is one thing their employers can do to keep them in their jobs. This shows that if you offer a basic benefits package and competitive rate, but your competitor offers just a few more perks, then your employees are liable to switch.

How else can you show your commitment to your people without actually investing in them? The answer is that you cannot.

That is why providing competitive packages can save you money, time, and headaches down the road. Keep your employees close and give them every prop they need to succeed. When you do this, you are bound to improve your employee retention.

Employee Retention

The main goal here for your company needs to be employee retention. We will talk more in detail about this in the next section. If you do not care about hiring and letting go over and over again, then this chapter was not for you. But if you have even an inkling about wanting to help your teams, then you need to take this into consideration.

It used to be that a job was merely a job.

You went to the office, and then went home and did not think about it until you came back the following morning. You could leave work behind and focus on your hobbies, family, and anything else that you wanted to spend your time on. Now, jobs have turned into careers that manage most of our lifestyles.

Even if you cannot see the direct link from a task to an outcome, the connections are there. Exercise is a good example in that you can see the action being taken and one expected outcome is better flexibility, mobility, and muscle growth. There are more outcomes though that will be related such as improved mental health and cognitive ability. This remains the same through much that we do, whether in the office or outside of it.

Forward Motions

Company culture continues to grow more important to hiring and retaining employees every year, just like a quality benefits package. Your teams will collaborate better and work harder when you treat them well. With this in mind, you need to consider the benefits and incentives provided in your organization now. Are they what your people need? Is it what they want? It is time to evaluate how well you are actually supporting everyone inside and outside of those office doors.

Step One: Review Past Benefits

Think over your past roles with the afforded privileges and provided incentives.

Even if this is your first full-time role with benefits, you need to complete a personal review of what you have received and how it has affected you. Consider the perks you have enjoyed and wanted along with those you did not care for. Maybe some do not impact you now, but could they in the future? Think about the past benefits you have received and what mattered most to you.

Step Two: Seek Out Employee Feedback

Connect with coworkers to see their thoughts on current benefits.

Talk with or send out a survey to your coworkers specifically outside of HR and leadership to learn their opinion on the current benefits package. Discover what they like, dislike, desire, and what is not working for them. Additionally, learn if the process of using these benefits has caused them any issues. When you connect with your coworkers, learn the pain points and how you can support them in their situations.

Step Three: Research Ideal Benefits

Work with the right people to build a game plan to improve their benefits.

Whether it is more incentives or different ones, whether you can make the change now or a year down the road, look for ways to positively impact your coworkers' benefits. Collaborate with your HR and leadership teams to find money in the budget along with ideas from Step Two in order for you to spend the money in the right manner.

This overall process may take weeks, even months to make it through all three steps. And even then, there may be more work that requires additional time. However, that is not a good enough excuse to delay this any longer. In fact, it just becomes clearer that you need to start right away to help your team.

Following through with this process will show your team that you are committed to them and their effort in the organization. The sooner you make these positive changes for your teams, the more successful they will become.

Part 2

Hiring Culture

Chapter Five

Gerald was the CEO of a busy company. They were beginning to grow but their turnover rates remained high: he was constantly needing to fill positions. Lacking the insights to understand his situation, he brought me on board to solve their problem.

I reviewed the HR strategies and helped implement them to ensure the onboarding process was properly organized so that it would be ready for new employees coming in. We worked on improving the hiring culture. Documents were prepared, and the onboarding process was reorganized. With everything in place, I believed we would be ready for the next new hire.

However, my plan did not work out when they recruited their next employee.

The CEO refused to use our newly implemented strategies. I tried to tell him that by ignoring what he thought was *red tape*, he was causing twice as many problems. His personal decisions were impacting the company when he stepped outside of the hiring

HR is *Sexy*

culture. It complicated everything for their HR team and left the recruit confused. Gerald excused himself saying that he did not believe he was doing anything wrong because that is how he had always done it; because he was the CEO, he could make the final call.

His resistance to change and the refusal to see the damage he caused meant his employees were leaving their jobs at his company because of his stubbornness. Complaints about his actions were made but ignored. The atmosphere at the company continued to worsen without processes established and maintained to ensure employees stayed on.

I tried to sit him down for a serious conversation. We had a "Come to Jesus" moment as I explained the situation. There was a clear connecting line from his choices to the results he was seeing. But he would not acknowledge this. He could not believe that he had ever been wrong. The hiring culture we created was ignored, which meant teamwork was crumbling without a chance for growth.

Every company has its own unique culture. Their hiring and company culture are specially created for the brand, allowing coworkers to come together and work toward the company goal.

I tried my best to create a healthy and dynamic system for Gerald's company. If the processes we created had been followed, then new employees would know they were joining a company that listened to, cared for, and understood them.

But the CEO's ideas of supporting new employees were riddled with favoritism, luck, and a serious lack of clarity. He gave people mixed messages and preferred his own opinion over facts. It made for an inauthentic, problematic, and unnecessarily complicated hiring culture.

Gerald was looking for a solution without putting in the effort and without the consideration of HR and his teams. I have seen this attitude in all levels of management, especially within the C-Suite. It is a dangerous and unhealthy way of managing an organization. He believed that because of his position, he knew best. Though Gerald said he wanted to improve the situation, he was not committed to doing whatever it would take.

I left because I could not do anything if he was not willing to change his mindset and put his people first. As far as I know, nothing changed once I left. It was unfortunate that there was nothing I could do.

We cannot help someone who does not want to be helped.

As an outside resource, it is my job to step in to help your organization. My focus lies in building cohesion between everyone in their roles and the company's goal. I am not there to do the work for you, but my team and I try to help you see clearly to create personalized solutions for every problem.

However, we cannot do anything if you ignore the evidence.

I was brought there to bring change. Employees struggled to get their work done through complicated systems and compliance issues were rising everywhere. Through my observation, I found that there were huge training opportunities that were being missed. There were numerous client complaints, pending court sanctions, and employee relations issues.

Essentially, this business was struggling.

The solution I provided had been reasonable. I built a training program that segmented progressive leadership. It started with new hires and moved up to leadership. Employees had to take these courses to move to the next step in the lifecycle of employment. We began with simple lessons and finished with more advanced training.

It is not enough to pull employees or leaders into a singular training session where you have them sit for an hour and listen to you lecture them. You need to have a process that everyone uses and can trust. Gerald wanted to skip important steps to show they were a "laid back company" and throw people into projects they were not yet equipped to handle.

When it comes to establishing a hiring culture, you have to be prepared to create a lasting system and continue to maintain it. A company needs to be consistent in its training processes and procedures. It is possible to establish a personal touch that does just this. While doing so, this needs to be done in an orderly manner that supports the company and will not hinder progress or employee growth.

There are boundaries that should be pushed and people that should not be pushed. The best way to bring your team together is not by pulling them every which way. Instead, we have to meet them where they are.

Employees join your company because they want to do their job. They want to succeed with your team and with your leadership. It is important to support them from the very beginning in the hiring process so that they are equipped with what they need to thrive while at your company.

Leaders want to do right by their people and employees want to do right by the company. Professionals want a chance to grow, and a company should desire that as well. Potential is just waiting to be put to use in the workplace. Thousands of companies prefer to hire from within because they have already laid the groundwork with those they are working within their departments.

Do you want to train a leader? Then go to them!

Be aware of their working environment and spend some time in their world. Study their processes and how they like to work. Learn what makes their position important, learn what makes them unique, and train as you go. Perfect moments do not just appear; they are made.

Employees need to know you care. Spending time learning their position is a great way to train them because when an employee knows you care, they start to work harder.

I know what you are going to say: *"Sorry, but I just do not have the time."*

That is not a good enough excuse. Truthfully, no excuse is beyond reproach when it comes to installing an uplifting culture in the company. There is no perfect solution. You cannot ignore the root of the problem like Gerald and hope for a miracle.

You need to make time. It is as simple as that. If you want to build your career and your organization, then you need to build up your people. Training equips leaders and employees with the skills necessary to successfully complete their jobs.

I do not, nor will I ever, believe that employees inherently go to work every day ready to purposefully do a bad job.

However, if your employees are not given the training they need, they will do the bare minimum to keep their position. They will struggle and do their best but cannot meet the standards you expect without help. These employees will not help the organization grow or develop to be successful, but rather continue with just meeting the status quo.

Time must be made for your people. When you put them first, your people will know that they are important and will strive for success.

Prioritize Your Hiring Process

Leaders and HR need to do better to prioritize their team members. A company needs communication and collaboration for them to move forward in meeting their deadlines and client expectations. They need people willing and able to accomplish their goals. If you want good people on your team, then you need to be prepared to put in the effort.

One of the best ways to provide this type of support is to give it at the beginning. This support should not be given to just anyone, but to the right candidates who can be the right employees for you. Before a professional has even joined the team, they should know what to expect.

Hire right the first time.

Hiring is not an easy process and should not be seen as such. New programs and strategies are being created every year. Some of them will work and some will not. Each company will be different. There is a balance between streaming it for ease and making it too complicated for anyone to weed through.

When you want to find the best talent in your pile of resumes, first look at the team you have already built.

Note their soft skills and character traits that have become invaluable to their team and the company. What do you love most about them? What makes them stand out as the top talent? When you discover what it is that makes them so successful, mark down those traits and abilities so that you can match them with potential recruits during the hiring process.

Take an example with Jason, the top marketing employee at an agency. He spends the majority of his time researching trends, creating new ideas, sharing his discoveries with his team, and training new staff. He is creative, a thinker, and inclusive. His whole personality is about growing himself, his team, and the company. The soft skills he puts to use the most are great communication and leadership, with his interpersonal skills. We can break those skills down into personal branding, team building, listening, and emotional maturity.

These are the handful of traits that make Jason

such an excellent employee. Once you can find similar traits in your top employees, you can note them down as the resumes are reviewed and interviews are started so you can look for these traits.

Of course, this is not to say that technical skills are not relevant or important. Just because someone has an optimistic attitude, it is not always the best or only reason to hire at your company. Many positions in the world require experience and technical skills, such as positions in a hospital or judicial court.

The trick is to balance soft skills against hard skills, with a bigger focus on the former. You can teach or train someone to have those specific technical skills that you need so badly in your office. But you cannot train someone to be a good human being.

Just because a talented individual can do their job does not mean that they will help the culture in your office to thrive and produce results. Rather, it can do the opposite. You risk losing a lot more if you hire people who only have hard skills and not soft ones.

Take a look at the talent in the NFL. Tom Brady was drafted 199th in the 2000 NFL draft because he had very limited football skills at the time. The following year, he took over Drew Bledsoe to become the greatest quarterback of our time. He lacked technical skill when he was first drafted, but he had the desire, the drive, and the determination to get to where he wanted to go. In contrast, Johnny Manziel was a trophy-winning and skilled college quarterback, drafted 22nd in the 2014 NFL draft. But he is already out of the game less than five years later because his soft skills were too weak compared to his technical skills.

We need to balance out our priorities to discover the type of character that we need in the company. It becomes a lot easier to hire right when you know just what type of person you are looking for.

People Process Improvement

Your hiring process should not be overly complicated. Having seen people jump through hoops in taking out time and even money in their attempt to find a new position, I have noticed that companies rarely offer such respect or kindness in return. Even having a five-step process or longer tends to be too lengthy.

When you prioritize your people, they will prioritize you in return.

While in the middle of the hiring process, make sure you are presenting your company truthfully and in a positive manner. This is an important glimpse for potential employees to see. They are interviewing you as well to see if the role would be a good fit for them. This can be done through conversations regarding expectations and the next step in the process if everything is going well.

Make sure that the people you are looking to hire are properly educated on the job expectations.

A company should be honest and transparent with their employees if they expect the same from said employees. There should be no secrets during the interviews and especially during their onboarding process.

One of the fastest ways to lose team members is by not being upfront with them.

Talented people know their limits as well as their boundaries. They know what they can do and cannot do. A company should never hire someone and attempt to push them past that point. Professionals know they will not be successful in certain situations. Telling your employees they should be prepared for one scenario but giving them another to struggle through is setting the employee and company up for failure.

Early in my career, I took a position at a national retailer as an HR Department Supervisor. The ad and interview entailed requirements and reviews of HR-related tasks and abilities. I was additionally told I would not have to work weekends.

When offered the role, I was thrilled. I spent two weeks eagerly learning the HR systems and meeting the team.

But then they suddenly assigned me to front desk customer service.

When I asked about the surprising change, the store manager explained that my HR work would only be necessary for half the week, and I would spend the other half working retail. He added that I would also be working that very weekend. Either there had been lies or miscommunication because I had never been warned about this before. As a single mother, that was not a possibility for me to manage those hours. Suddenly, I could not afford this job I had been so thrilled about because they had not been honest with me.

As the professional world continues to advance, one situation to keep in mind is how HR should actively be searching out diversity. To attract and retain top talent, you must look outside your 'comfort zone' of obvious candidates with clear-cut experience.

Talent comes through all ethnicities, cultures, races, religions, etc. Disregarding someone for one of these reasons is extremely problematic. Not only do you play into supporting stereotypes and deeply flawed social structural issues, you also risk losing out on great talent.

Everyone brings a different set of skills with a fresh vision to their role that can boost your company more than you could have expected. In doing so, they can help attract additional top talent in the future.

When I was helping to hire for an accounting position, I ran into the problem of trying to please two different leaders. The new leader of the department was active, loud, and opinionated. His recruiting technique was to hire more people like him.

However, the CFO disagreed and wanted someone quiet who would keep their head down. They did not want any changes made to the status quo, effectively burning that mentality into the new leader and everyone else who came through the door. Few changes were ever made in that department because they were not welcome. This kept them weighed down with outdated thought processes and strategies that would ultimately affect their department in a negative manner.

The hiring culture you create will fluctuate based on the team members who arrive and how they leave. Change can be considered good, and it can open the door to more possibilities, but only if it is properly invited to be part of the group.

A company can stand out against its competition and attract top talent with soft and hard skills when they build healthy relationships and have transparency in the hiring process.

If you struggle to stand out, you can start reaching out to people by building a conversation to establish a relationship with others. You need to be honest about your company and the possibilities, which is possible to do without being negative or desperate. Emphasize the philanthropy within your company, showcasing the causes that you, and even your clients, are involved in.

Doing these small things can show others that you are committed to creating change and really are looking to hire the top talent.

When you are looking to improve your hiring process and build with the best talent, you should be prepared to compensate them in an appreciative manner. Even if people come to love your company and their team, not everyone can afford to work for fun.

Top talent does not come cheap in paycheck, benefits, or culture. You will lose out if you elect to settle with cheap rates.

Additionally, it may not matter how much you pay if your employees do not like the company culture you have established. In the chapter's first story, I spoke of Gerald who made wayward decisions whenever he felt like it and ignored the hiring culture that set team members up for success. Companies and people both need more structure to survive and thrive in the workplace.

If your work environment is unsupportive, ineffective, or intolerant in any way, then you will have a revolving door of talent coming and going. To attract the best talent in your industry, you should evaluate your workplace culture, your pay practices, and the various benefits offered like those we discussed in Chapter Three.

The managing founder of the law firm I worked at spent years trying to attract a rockstar COO to join the company. Eventually, the timing paid off and the right benefits package was offered so that the professional joined our firm.

But that was not enough. Not too long after coming on board, problems arose.

The executive culture at this firm was atrocious. It affected the new COO along with the other leaders, rolling off to the staff level. There was no recognition and no honesty, equating a lack of trust and support. The hiring culture had presented a great opportunity to the COO, but not an honest one. Because of these issues, the COO was unable to make a positive impact and they were unable to get their work done and so they left.

Ultimately, this COO was successful in their earlier endeavors as well as the opportunities that came afterward. In regard to the law firm, it continued to struggle.

Every step of the recruitment process is important to help build trust between you and the new employees, while making sure they are given everything they need to succeed in the office. Whether it is giving them equipment or helping them learn a few more skills, you need to be there to support them.

The onboarding process may be marked as complete, but it does not mean that you just abandon your employees to figure things out on their own. Throughout their time at your organization, it is important to continue building them up for success. If not, you are essentially creating that revolving door of people coming and going, a hire-to-fire process.

Fix That Retention Rate

Hiring people takes time, effort, and money. Sometimes the process takes so long that the extra work is put on someone's plate to handle while someone else is recruited. Having to handle several jobs at once is stressful and time-consuming, ultimately leading employees to burn out. Give a person a job and they will excel. Give them a second job, and they will begin to lose their balance.

There is a trick to hiring right the first time, but that does not mean the job is done. The next step is to keep them in their role. Though it may seem easy to simply let people go when there is a problem at the company, as portrayed in several of the stories in this book, doing this often only adds more problems to everyone's plate.

The subconscious habit of "hire to fire" needs to change to "save as many as we can."

If you are concerned about your organization possibly needing help in the recruiting process, then ask yourself questions within a few key areas. Be honest and refer to data for anything you might be hesitant to personally decide upon.

1. **What is your company's turnover rate?** See if this is prone to a certain department or specific manager, looking for any patterns. Once you identify the truth behind the excessive turnover, you can begin identifying any training gaps, review failures, lack of directions, and job expectations.

2. **Do you have any employee complaints?** Whether it is through HR, anonymous surveys, or online reviews, see how people submit them and a strategy for how your company handles them. Has the policy been applied consistently and if not, why not? Once you understand where employees believe their problems stem from, you can begin revising strategies and refreshing processes so they are advantageous instead of problematic.

3. **Are there any company- or employee-related compliance issues?** Review to make sure your company is updated on mandated requirements made by your state and the federal government. An audit can negatively impact employees as well as the company. Look around to see how well your HR could pass an audit if you had one today. Once you review all potential compliance issues, you can begin updating your systems, training team members on their knowledge gaps, and review your strategies for employee support.

These are just three questions that you can ask yourself to make sure you and your people are truly supporting your employees.

Training Right

One of the best ways to retain and support your employees is to continue training them. This includes HR and leadership as well, to help them to keep growing. This can be inclusive of a mentorship program or built as something else.

At least 68% of professionals desire to learn or train in the workplace. The argument that these employees are learning and not working is invalid because this learning process is actively meant to help them become better employees.

Training should be made extensive to the point of an organization having its own unique and specialized training program in place. Such a program could help employees to grow in their skills as well as build a better understanding of the company. Whether it is simple or complex, *training should always be a priority.* At this time, one out of two companies in America does not have a formal training strategy in place for every employee. This is something that needs to change.

Employees will begin to create their own cultures, departments will build their own processes, and leaders will work out of sync with others if proper training protocols are not put in place at a company. Training helps all employees to reach the same level of understanding with the company's mission. When training becomes part of the workplace culture, it helps everyone to work in the same direction.

Employees feel better and work better when they have clear direction.

It is imperative that leaders are continually leading and educating in the same manner. If your leaders do not do this, employees will get frustrated and confused. That slows down production, builds contention, and causes damage to teams and work efforts.

As mentioned at the beginning of this chapter, the main obstacle that companies face in providing successful training is time. That is the number one reason why employees do not invest in learning.

Leaders also often feel that they do not have time to make training a real priority or they do not have the time to partake in well-rounded, hands-on training opportunities. When this reason is used to explain the lack of training, employees take on the same attitude--meaning employees default to feeling too busy to properly participate in training programs that could be extremely beneficial.

People want to learn whether they realize it or not.

Employees want to do their job well and leaders try to guide their teams and the company in the right direction. By providing the right opportunities, teams will work better together to meet the bottom line.

Personal experience has taught me that building others in this manner provides more opportunities than just sitting sound and hoping for the best. Even having team members support and train each other, no matter their position, can help build better communication and collaboration across the departments.

There is often the concern that by teaching each other one's skills, they are then shutting themselves out of their position. Leaders often suppose that if two employees share the same skills, then they only need one of those employees. Neither of these situations should ever take place because hard and soft skills are always different for each person in how the skills are put to use. To remove one employee is to add a whole workload to another's plate which will slow them down.

At my practice, I teach leaders to devote time so they can train and build up others at their company. When this is done, more tasks are completed successfully and quickly, company profits grow, and everyone gains skills that make them more valuable and helpful in their role.

Successful training creates a successful organization.

When employees are trained, any team member helping to train will also gain invaluable experience. Building others up has given me hands-on experience in leading others. This provides valuable insights and teaches me what more I can do to succeed, effectively helping me to secure better leadership opportunities in organizations.

Training should also be seen as a chance to network with others. Whether it is within your own organization or with another, we can learn from everyone around us. In the past, I have had leaders that would task me with new responsibilities and duties so I could cultivate new skills and continue growing.

In order for a company to maintain an upward trajectory, employees need to continue doing more and learning more.

Training can help drive the success of a company. Without it, there runs a high risk of lost opportunities and negative team experiences. Professionals who refuse to acknowledge the benefits of continued training in their career are just one of many red flags that you should keep an eye out for.

Red Flags

In my business of supporting companies through HR strategies and processes, I have grown familiar with red flags and what needs to be done to correct unhealthy and unproductive situations.

One of the biggest red flags I find in a company is high turnover.

These happen most often in organizations that lack a good training program. Without training and similar support, employees feel stranded and there are bound to be more mistakes in work products. This leads to people leaving and that is when I know something is wrong. It means people are giving up and looking for a better workplace.

You can see this, especially in the recruiting process. If a new hire leaves within the first thirty days of employment, they are leaving because of job expectations. If a new hire leaves within the first sixty to ninety days, then they are leaving because of leadership and training-related issues. When employees leave a company after those ninety days, their main reason for leaving will either be money, benefits, growth potential, or leadership. Sometimes it can be several of those issues that have continued to negatively affect a professional.

Though we have already dedicated an earlier section to leadership, I need to reiterate that one of the biggest complaints that employees make will be in regards to the leadership team. When employees continue to complain, especially about a particular leader, then there are serious issues that cannot continue to go unresolved.

This means that you need to take a good, long look at that leader.

Consider their skillset as a People Leader or Process Leader. Ask yourself if they have been provided adequate training on the leadership culture of the business. Can you tell if they have been taught to handle conflict resolution?

This is just another reason why training is so important. Often when one person leaves the company, there is still a workload left on the table that suddenly gets transferred onto someone else's plate. Usually, that person is lacking training and needs support to learn how to juggle the additional work until it is handed off again.

The lack of succession planning is another red flag that I have seen throughout companies that I have worked with. Often when one person leaves, leaders believe that their current team can handle that extra work.

That is not usually the case.

It is also a problem to promote someone to that now-empty role without helping them to have prepared to get to that point in their career. A promotion is an exciting opportunity, but you are setting people up for failure when you do not properly prepare them.

Look at your teams and question how well different types of emergencies would be handled. When you search for gaps, consider what you can do to fill them. Both leadership and HR have a responsibility to support training.

That is not to say that all employees will take to training well. While the red flags I have mentioned address the companies, there are red flags found within our employees as well.

Whether an employee is prideful, comfortable, or stubborn, sometimes they are not interested in training programs or more lessons on how to do their job better. This happens. It is our job to do our best to try and help them before taking any drastic action.

Start these conversations off in a pleasant manner. Non-coachable employees need to know what they are doing well. When a leader or HR person has a conversation with an employee who is not coachable, they should start out with praise on what the employee is doing correctly. It is important that this employee does not feel like a failure.

Once you have offered up the praise you can lead in with areas of suggestion.

Generally, an employee will look at this as a goal to meet and will want to be praised again not even realizing it was an opportunity. Employees who will not take coaching that way may need a little tough love and hard lessons on just doing things their own way whether it is removing some of their responsibilities or holding constructive feedback meetings to give them the opportunity to be coached. To help you know what to look out for in such resistant employees, consider some of these traits:

- **Non-coachable employees: stubborn, argue against advice, disregard new programs, create excuses to delay deadlines and make the same mistakes over and over again.**
- **Coachable employees: good listeners, ask questions, accept change, enjoy new opportunities, meet deadlines, and make progress in work relationships and tasks.**

This will not always be accurate, but these are helpful guidelines to look out for in your team members. We should seek to understand the people around us and as we do, we will learn how we can help them and work together. This teaches us to open our minds, become more flexible, and grow professionally.

Hiring Culture

When you create your company's hiring culture, you are bringing to life the values that the organization is built on. This is the first introduction to the company culture that new employees experience as they are recruited, interviewed, and onboarded.

Sometimes the hiring culture and company culture are not entirely in sync. This is usually harmless so long as the values are linked in one way or another. To be polar opposites is to lead your new employee from one situation to the next quickly, hoping they can keep up. However, that is unfair to your people who just want to do a good job.

Because of this, it is best to ensure that the hiring culture is similar to the company culture so that it can be a gateway for new employees to walk easily into their new roles.

One of the most important steps to achieve this cohesion is to ensure that everyone is involved.

HR needs to know who to engage during the hiring process for each new role. Leadership at all levels needs to be extensively trained on the company's mission, vision, and values. This can be done through interviews, training, and other strategies. Once management is clearly informed, the staff needs to follow in the same, or a similar, program.

As the time comes to bring new employees to join the team, their potential leaders and team members should be included in the onboarding process. In the right situations, some should even be brought on during recruitment. This allows professionals to draw close in welcoming, training, mentoring, and guiding new employees in their new roles. It teaches teamwork as well as inclusion, which has recently become a popular core value for companies looking to grow and better support their people.

Just taking the first step to making people comfortable in your company culture creates a sense of camaraderie where people have a chance to feel seen, heard, and respected. Once you manage to direct your organization in the right direction and are bringing on board the right people, then you have begun creating a promising and efficient hiring culture.

You can continue to build on your culture in innovative ways. As discussed, the best way to manage a company is to have the right people working alongside you. Putting extra effort into your current recruitment practices can do that.

America has made it illegal to discriminate against people for many reasons, yet even now many current and static strategies do little to actively improve their processes in recruiting diverse professionals. *We can do better if we will put in the effort.* Employees who come in with their different backgrounds, whether due to ethnicity, education, or culture, allow a company to utilize ideas from a different and fresh perspective. This results in the ability for the company to grow, often diversifying their products and lines with innovative employee support.

I once worked with a client who was struggling with their stagnant sales. Seeing their tenured and experienced staff who had been for many years, I could see that they needed something new in the office.

More specifically, they needed *someone* new.

They had run out of ideas on how to improve their processes and after some consideration, they were willing to put in the time and money to hire interns from the local university. The idea did not excite these industry-leaders who had been in the business for many years, but we found three Juniors for a summer program and brought them onboard. Each intern took on their own market research project the first month and then combined the research to collaborate with each other. At the conclusion of their internship, they brought forward ideas about how the company could innovate and grow.

Our results exceeded my expectations. The entire leadership team was on board with the new suggestions. Not only did their revenue go up by 30% that first year, but all three interns were eventually recruited for full-time jobs. This company continues to run a summer internship so they can keep growing.

Practices like these can go a long way in building up the right team and improving employee retention.

When you are flexible, transparent, and communicative within your company culture, you build a healthy and successful workplace. The healthier your workplace, the more your retention rate will improve. Teams will collaborate and build better together. And the company will flourish.

Forward Motions

The hiring culture is vital to a company's growth. From the get-go, it shows employees what to expect. It is a type of support system to understand everyone's responsibilities and the potential at the workplace. This is a chance for you to create positive and lasting change. Study what has worked well in your company and see how other successful organizations have improved their processes. When you begin to revitalize the programs at work, make sure you start at the beginning with your hiring culture.

Step One: Analyze Your Hiring Strategy

Review your recruitment pipeline for gaps and possible improvements.

When you review the last dozen hires, look at how they made it through your hiring process and how well the system successfully hired the right people. Mark down what sort of hiccups you might have run into, any steps that may have caused delays, and the steps that worked well. Review not just the process, but how your people work together through your process along with any online programs that are utilized to consider their lasting benefits.

Step Two: Collect Data About Your Onboarding Process

Track down information to better understand the new-employee experience.

Perhaps you know what it is like to hire professionals at your company, but you must learn what it is like for people being hired. Once you have reviewed your process, seek out input from your employees. You can put together surveys, questionnaires, and other forms to invite people hired through the current system to fill out and share their experiences. This will give you an intimate look at where other issues may reside.

Step Three: Strategize For a Better System

Based on the first two steps, plan how you can create a better hiring culture and system.

Once you have collected your information and analyzed the data, now is your chance to make a positive impact by updating your company hiring process. There is always room for improvement. And to provide a great hiring culture, you need to be on your toes and ready to make some changes when necessary.

Establishing a flexible and supportive hiring culture may sound intimidating. But by taking it step by step, and including the right people into supporting it, our workplaces can be much better suited for each employee that joins the team. This helps people to prepare for working alongside each other for a mutual purpose.

If you want to have an efficient and cooperative workplace, making sure you have the right people onboard will make all the difference. Create the ideal hiring culture to attract top talent. This will allow you to find and recruit professionals with the right skills to make a valuable impact.

Chapter Six

In the 1980s, the Frito-Lay brand was beginning to struggle. A janitor was working in their Southern California factory by the name of Richard Montanez, a man who had never finished middle school. He worked for minimum wage in the factory with the belief that no matter what he did, he would always do his best.

The few hard–or *technical*–skills he had were concentrated in cleaning up the various rooms and offices, finishing his work so everything was in order and tidy.

But hard skills are not the only skills that can be use. Montanez was also an observant person, a family man, and he was determined to succeed.

There are a few variations of his story, but this is the gist of what happened. During this time, he realized that the company was missing out on a large market in his area. Thousands of Latinos live near the Mexico border, and they are well-known for their love of and talent with spices. While there were international brands of spicy chips, Frito-Lay did not have any.

This is where Montanez came in. He already worked hard with his technical skills in cleaning and mopping. His soft skills were inclusive of curiosity, determination, and integrity. The man saw this gap and took his chance. He took some undusted Cheetos from the factory home with him. Reminded of elote, the popular Mexican street corn snack, Montanez covered his Cheetos with similar spices.

Of course, the story does not end here. Montanez knew that he had created something good that could greatly benefit both the company and its customers. He put his soft skills to use as he called up the CEO to let him know what he had done.

It did not take long before he was invited to make an official pitch to the board.

The meeting went well and in 1992, Flamin' Hot Cheetos made its national release. Frito-Lay had only three Cheeto products at that time and has now created over twenty varieties. The product continues to sell to this day and Richard Montanez rose through the ranks with his success to become Vice President of Multicultural Sales for Frito-Lay's holding company.

Richard Montanez set a clear example of how diverse skills can be put together in a professional's career so that they benefit the employee, the company, and the customers.

As discussed in the prior chapter, having a mix of soft and hard skills can be invaluable in any capacity. They can help to improve teamwork, create better processes, and produce impressive results. For HR to only hire and for leadership to only focus on the hard skills is practically shooting yourself in the foot. If you are not careful, you are also hurting your coworkers and the company.

Highlighting the various skill sets of your employees allows you to utilize everything within your grasp. It is difficult to fight a battle when you have one hand strapped behind your back. Just the same, it would be cruel to ignore the effort that your teams are willing to put in to achieve their tasks. Everyone within your organization should be able to access their skills that will help them to work better and bring about potential results.

This is not just for your employees. You and the other professionals in leadership and HR need to be putting your skills to use.

The more you use them, the more these skills will grow and help you to gain new skills along the way. Everyone has a variety of talents. There are those who have invested in learning hard technical skills like computer programming, writing, and public speaking. And there are those who have spent time focused on learning management and communication skills.

Every person juggles a unique combination of hard and soft skills that not only help them become who they are meant to be but helps them to make progress on their tasks and goals.

History has a bad reputation for singling out hard skills as the one necessary ability for a hard worker or a leader to have. As the workplace changes and roles are changed up every couple of years, spending more time focusing on soft skills will become necessary. They cannot be a side factor of something that is brought up at the end of an interview.

When recruiting, talent specialists should be paying close attention to the different types of skills that are being brought up during the hiring process.

This can be especially valuable for the occasions when professionals have decided to switch careers and move into a different industry. Just because someone is not an expert coder does not mean they should not be given the right type of opportunity to start coding in a junior position or taking on a few small tasks with their current workload.

If they are self-aware and determined, among their other skills, then there is a fair chance that they can quickly learn to succeed in their new role. Professionals are more than capable of applying their unique skill sets to every position that they take upon themselves.

Transferable Skill Sets

While a truck driver may have a hard time switching from a job driving on the road to taking a desk in an office as an assistant, this does not mean that the truck driver would be bound to fail in the new position.

Hard and soft skills, albeit mostly the latter, can be considered transferable when they are moved from one role to another.

In this modern era, more professionals are switching their work in industries and roles more than ever before. No longer does someone hire on and stay in the same position until they are ready to retire. That has become the minority of employees. The average expectancy for someone to stay in one job is now less than five years. Many will often attempt to find a similar role in title and responsibilities. But a few more professionals each year make up their minds to switch between two vastly different roles.

Just because a potential employee has not worked in this role does not mean that they have nothing to bring to the table. When you are working with HR and the appropriate leader about filling a new position, a review should be made addressing the needs filled through the role. One should consider gathering a list of potential soft skills that would be beneficial while also leaving room for other skills to present themselves in the interviews. This will allow recruiters and managers to interview a diverse collection of potential employees who can all bring their specialties to the table.

Through the interview process, a company may find an unlikely and extraordinary recruit--possibly one they had not realized.

It is often the unexpected professionals who can bring about great change. There is an unlimited number of people like Richard Montanez who are eagerly looking for the opportunity to make a positive impact on the world around them. When you take those chances, you are helping yourself and the company that you work for.

Such transferable skills will be beneficial when the people on your team take on new responsibilities and receive promotions. Use these skills as a guide to tell you which team members are going to be able to help you in certain ways and on particular projects. You will know better about who to promote into leadership roles, how you can utilize others across departments, and you will be able to find the right people to lead new initiatives.

These skills are a part of who these people are through and through. Professionals will try to use them to the best of their abilities, and HR and leadership need to support that.

Soft skills are inherently part of who we are as people.

It is difficult to change the core of who a person is. In that same sense, it is nearly impossible to separate people from these soft skills. They help make people inherently who they are, which impacts the way they work and interact with everyone around them.

Trying to remove a soft skill from someone, or asking them not to use it, is like asking someone to not be themselves. We should not seek to backtrack someone's progress from the person they have spent a lifetime becoming. Instead, we should be putting those skills to good use.

Whether or not they have been in the same field for all of their career, it does not matter.

What matters is how much effort and drive your employees are willing to put in to do their best. When your team gives it their all, then you are bound to move forward in leaps and bounds.

Implementing Programs

Hiring someone because of their soft skills does not mean you should leave them stranded in their job to pick up where they are. They still deserve time and attention to help them get to the point they need to in order to do their best and achieve ideal results.

A company should implement programs that will help its employees cultivate both hard and soft skills.

As we discussed, employees both need and deserve training.

There are great programs already created to help professionals and there is always room for more. From conferences to online courses, everyone should be given the opportunity to keep on growing. This is ultimately a benefit for companies when they have intelligent employees building growth within their own skill sets because that will reflect positively on their company.

Hard skills are easily teachable and measurable. This can include learning new software, selling to new clients, and restocking shelves. In contrast, soft skills are more difficult to teach but are not impossible.

It is easier to build new soft skills than to change out old ones. Thus, when it comes to teaching skills like diplomacy, etiquette, and communication, it can be more difficult. But with hard skills, they are not impossible to teach or to learn. All of these skills can help someone to be a good employee. By providing opportunities for your employees to learn such skills, they will handle their workload better than ever before.

There are many ways to go about bringing them into the workplace. But the basic workflow should be followed:

1. Leadership and HR need to commit to their program.
2. Communicate with employees to make sure everyone is aware.
3. Introduce the program–with the leaders in charge–and offer motivation.
4. Once the program is underway, collect feedback.

Many like to sidestep that final step and consider the first three good enough. Many programs are instituted without feedback or review. It is easy to work through a plan and then let it go once you are done so that you never need to look at it again.

This should never happen. Improvement in our skills takes dedicated effort and time from those receiving and giving the help.

There are many programs in existence now that have been created to help professionals. There are online programs to teach and refine hard skills like presentation outlines, coding, and organization techniques. People have also put together in-person programs for public speaking, etiquette, and management support. More programs are created every year so it would be more than possible for any company to invest in company accounts to teach their employees.

If that is not preferred, your company can create its own programs.

This will take time so that the right people can be assigned to oversee the creation and management of these said programs. Once they are put in place, they will need to do their research and reviews with team members to see just what type of program is necessary to fill the gaps of knowledge. Then they will need to prepare the program by knowing what the end goal is for everyone who takes it. Working backward, these professionals can build milestones and eventually have something put together to benefit their coworkers.

One of the ways that many companies are beginning to offer support in developing hard skills and expanding on their soft skills is through continued education. By supporting an employee's tuition for a degree or certification, a company can earn their employee's trust and commitment. When finished, this employee will be better prepared for promotions and can do more to support their company and teams.

While there are many professionals who work well on their own, one of the best things about many programs is how it requires people to work together.

Whether it is by learning together or challenging one another to grow, having a small team of coworkers committed to finishing the program together can make all the difference in how well a program does.

This will reflect the employees' soft skills and hard skills by the end.

Even experts at the top of their field can use an opportunity to refresh their skill sets and learn from those around them. Then they can put these skills to use. Such an investment can boost a company to increase their profit and build better relationships with their clients.

Your teams already have a lot of potential. When you let them put that to use in implementing programs, you are giving your people the chance to put that potential to good use.

Setting Reasonable Expectations

As programs are implemented and your team members continue cultivating their skills, it is vital for leadership and HR to pay close attention.

Not only is feedback helpful in making sure that the right program has been created but looking for their suggestions and progress can instill confidence in their new growth.

New ideas will be brought to the table that should be taken seriously and their insights can make a big difference in updating strategies and creating solutions. As you do so, create an atmosphere where these new ideas are welcome so your team members can put their knowledge to use. Companies can make big claims about being open to such concepts, all the while ignoring all the suggestions that are being made.

Change should be one of the most constant attributes of your company.

Invite the change and the possibilities that come when your employees continue to improve their skills. By being prepared in advance when the programs are offered, leaders can create expectations for their desired outcome.

Setting reasonable expectations for your teams is important to helping them to do their jobs to the best of their abilities. These are already established as part of their job requirements in being professional, communicating with team members, and meeting the goals for the team and company.

These expectations will be unique for each company, learning program, and employee. By focusing on a few highlights addressing employee potential, you can set up guidelines on how the program affects your employee's working time and what you both expect to learn in the process.

Never expect the same results from different people.

Just as you hire people for their unique talents

and skill sets, you should never expect them to produce the same thing over and over again with one another. Expectations should be set, tailored to each individual. Evaluations can be created to be discussed between those employees and their leaders. It does not need to include anyone else unless they were directly involved in the process.

Expectations are for current employees, new hires, and their leaders. Such expectations can be a great benefit to professionals in helping them track progress within the workplace.

This can be done for soft and hard skills. As your employees continue working on their projects and long-term goals, they can decide on the skills that they want to strengthen and how that can be done. Leaders and HR can help them set these goals and expectations, working together in order to complete them.

Supporting employees who are improving their skill sets is an important role that leadership and HR handles for the company.

Instituting Balance

There is a need for balance when it comes to discussing and working on skill sets. As people choose to work on themselves and their professional abilities, it is important to institute balance in a person's personal and professional lives.

Firstly, you need to be able to find a balance in putting both types of skills to use.

There is a time and place for everything. Professionals are hired to complete a job based on their talents, and they need to make sure they can accomplish their work. Everyone should be encouraged to work on their skills while learning to use certain ones at certain times.

As professionals pick up new skills and refine those they already have, a company should ensure that their teams have the right type of access to training courses. Even for those seeking to pick up new skills in fields outside of their job role, this should be considered a welcome idea.

A diverse set of skills in a person can help them open new neurological pathways in thinking and bring new ideas to the table.

Whether an employee is wanting to pick up a new skill in their current field, one that would move them forward in their career, or something new outside of their field, their leaders such as yourselves should welcome such an opportunity. Your team will be better qualified in their roles, they will be more harmonized in their work together, and your company will be grateful to you for your support in the long run– just like your employees.

Different workloads and responsibilities call for different types of skills. A professional can spend one day focusing on their communication skills in countless meetings, only to spend the following workday coding and drafting documentation. All skill sets are important and may belong in different circumstances.

There may be employees who struggle to find the balance. This would open up the opportunity for HR to step in, within the support of leadership, in offering help. This can be done individually or on a larger scale through webinars, programs, or another form of support.

Secondly, there needs to be a balance between the learning and the workload.

Skills need to be utilized at the right time to be of use. Time spent in webinars and learning programs will need to be limited during the day. I have already stated that learning and training opportunities are important and must be considered part of a professional's workload.

However, that does not always mean that an entire workday should be dedicated to these learning opportunities. This will be greatly dependent on the current strategies and workload that each professional is working on with their leaders.

Some training may be more necessary, such as gaining certifications, and will require more time in the office. Then there will be other learning opportunities, like online programs, that should be more flexible and maneuvered around workloads. Professionals can work with their direct leadership in deciding what strategy will work best in order to balance their current task lists and their chance to learn.

Balance plays an important role within a person's life, no matter what they do or where they are. Taking this seriously in the workplace can greatly benefit professionals and companies alike. It is a chance to work together, grow together, and build together.

Forward Motions

Employees come into their positions with a skill set already in hand. These skills may be fresh or well-developed. Either way, the workplace is the perfect place to apply their talents and contribute to the company. Leaders and HR need to do everything they can to put these skills to a good purpose. As you work on this, make sure that you are considering your own skill sets and how to set up your teams for success.

Step One: Create a List of Your Skills

List the hard and soft skills that you use every day to evaluate how they help you.

Before you start evaluating others with their skills, take some time to review your own. You can consider those that you use in the workplace and those that you use elsewhere. How have they grown over the last couple of years? Are there any you feel that could be used more frequently? What other skills do you want to learn? Mark those that you use the most often and how they have helped to benefit you and your company.

Step Two: Review Hiring Process for Skills

Look over your hiring strategies to ensure you have made room for all skill sets.

Hiring processes are often automated in order to streamline the work and help hire people faster. However, there is a chance that these processes may have some gaps that are keeping you from hiring diverse and talented professionals who could greatly benefit the company. See where there could be room to discuss hard skills and soft skills during your hiring process.

Step Three: Establish Skill-Centered Goals

Help yourself and your company to succeed by reviewing potential skill sets.

Now is the time for you to look back at your list of skills to see what you could be working on in order to become a better professional. Find a skill that you know you can and should work on. As you do so, work with your recruiters to update your hiring system so it is more focused and personalized in hiring for each role. Without a human touch in the hiring process, you are bound to miss some great talent.

As you seek to hire and keep the right people on your teams, it is important to remember that people can only do as much good as you allow them to in the workplace. Hire people for their hard, technical skills as well as their soft ones. And if you want them to improve, then be prepared to give them the time and tools necessary for their growth. Giving people a chance can bring about impressive results.

Every employee is an investment that needs to be taken seriously in every type of workplace. Every person wants the chance to succeed and support their company. Giving these opportunities to your coworkers may be the difference between barely meeting expectations to exceeding expectations. Help them to develop their skill sets for potential, growth, and commitment.

Chapter Seven

Reputation is key to your hiring culture. My first HR position was in a prison. There was an incident there that stayed with me forever. That role taught me everything I needed to know and more about working with people and dealing with complicated situations. While I knew I wanted to work in HR, I encountered one of the worst incidents of inhumane treatment that led to my departure.

Jake was a tenured correctional officer for eight years. He came to work, did his job, and went home. One day, he got in between two inmates who were fighting, they were trying to beat each other with a lock in a sock (literally), and he was attempting to diffuse the situation. Jake calmed the men down and sent them back to their cells. Handling a situation like this required several steps and writing up an incident report.

Though he did his job, everything fell apart. Leadership viewed the video footage of the recorded incident and decided that he had used force. They said the palm of his hand slightly touched the shirt of the inmate, but it had not mentioned it in his report.

HR is *Sexy*

A mistake like this required Jake to be suspended pending an investigation and a disciplinary hearing.

The latter was scheduled for two weeks later on a Wednesday. The Tuesday before, our office received instruction from corporate to lay off ten percent of the entire workforce. Leadership immediately took action to mark down who they were letting go. Jake was on that list.

In my lower HR position, I handled confidential information but no control over the decisions. I saw the powers that be bring in Jake the following day for his disciplinary hearing, watching him beg for his job, crying, on his knees (he was telling them he just had a new baby). even though they all knew full well he had been terminated the day before. Nothing he could say or do would get him his job back.

This made me question my decision to work in HR. How could I spend the rest of my career doing something so cruel? This is not how I wanted to treat people. I went to my leader afterward to tell her how this situation concerned me.

She said, "Sometimes management has to make decisions that are not always popular, but we did the right thing."

Still not understanding, I asked, "Why did they not call him on Tuesday to let him know that he had been let go?"

The response I received was this: "He was entitled to his disciplinary hearing." Seeing my unhappy reaction, they asked, "What is wrong?"

"If Jake was entitled to a disciplinary hearing, why was he let go in the layoff?" I asked. "He was supposed to get his chance to defend himself, especially since he did nothing wrong."

My leader just shrugged. "That was just semantics, he was getting fired." This was not a satisfactory answer and when I tried to press the issue on why they would be so disrespectful and waste his time, I was told to drop the issue.

A few days later, I was called into the warden's office for a meeting where I was told, "Not to put nails in my coffin." Speaking to my leader like I had done was not permitted and it was more important to get work done than to worry about the people around me. Considering that was a key tenant to the role of HR, this is why I knew that I could not stay there.

The company began enforcing their nepotism policy. I had been hired there with everyone knowing my mom and brother worked there. The push back was obvious as nepotism began a much more obvious reign. This was the first time I had experienced retaliation in the workplace for speaking out as I had. It was not long before I left. Just to let you know, of all the relatives in this prison, I was the only person who was receiving push back and transfer warnings. All because I was asking questions.

As I said, this incident has stayed with me forever. It negatively affected several lives. Leadership had made irresponsible decisions that humiliated and hurt people.

This HR role taught me a wealth of knowledge in how to act and how not to act. I had been thrilled to learn the ropes and succeed in my career. I learned quickly and accepted the responsibilities. I was willing to put up with the constant flow of paperwork. I had thought I had a well-educated and cool boss. This had been a career I wanted to make for myself. The expectations I had set were reasonable in looking forward to learning and growing my skills while supporting the HR office. It is more than acceptable for employees and employers to set such expectations.

And we have a responsibility to act in a respectful manner. Offices need to operate at a certain level of human decency. I had thought this was widely accepted and well-known, but this HR office had lowered their standards to an unbelievable level.

As I began to get more involved with the day-to-day employee relations issues, I started to question my decision of joining the HR field. I could not put my finger on whether it was the leadership or the fact that every day it was something new.

We would constantly have problem after problem.

But there was a troublesome pattern that I had noticed. Our problems, you see, were not with the inmates, but the employees. Employees would leave after only a week in a position or major complaints were filed on a manager. It was a never-ending circus of chaos.

Hold yourselves and your company to professional and fair-minded standards.

To this day, I still cannot fathom someone's reasoning for disregarding human decency like they did that day. Jake did not deserve to be given false hope in that manner but should have been treated with respect. Even people who make mistakes deserve to be treated fairly.

Whether it was one person taking the lead in this decision process or all of them were in agreement, behavior like this should never be permitted in the workplace. Teamwork can bring about great results. However, too many hands in the cookie jar will get everyone stuck. As I have discussed in this book so far, HR can cause just as many problems as it can solve. There are a lot of nuances when it comes to compliance, workplace relationships, and employee engagement. These are issues that need to be taken seriously because they are bound to affect the people in the workplace and your external reputation that prevents you from recruiting and retaining top talent.

Whether it is within a company's HR department or within leadership wanting to make HR-related decisions, allowing such behavior is a recipe for disaster.

We must hold ourselves and our coworkers to a standard of respect for the rules as well as the people around us. There should never be room for nepotism, disrespect, or neglect in any type of workplace. One of the best ways to combat this is to focus on ensuring space for the human touch.

Working Without a Human Touch

Discussing the *human touch* bears repeating, especially when there may be confusion or ignorance surrounding the matter.

When discussing the human touch, it tends to be used in conversations for marketing and customer engagement. But often before you attract your clients and after some of them leave, you still have your employees. These people are not disposable. They have lives, feelings, desires, and are the core to helping your company succeed.

The inclusion of the human touch connotes the idea that everyone is seen as a human being and respected in a like manner. They are given fair opportunities, listened to when they have something to say, and should be provided the chance to succeed in their positions.

Your clients and employees may not be the same people. *But they are still people.* As you seek to understand and serve your clients to fulfill their needs, you need to be doing the same for your employees. We have discussed that providing comfortable benefits is a great way to show that your company cares for them.

However, if you really want to retain employees, especially the best of the best, then they need to be respected. Consider the benefits to be your hard skills and your respect as your soft skills.

Leaders and HR set expectations for the new hires they recruit and bring onto their teams. In a like manner, these new hires set expectations for their new coworkers. It is only by working together can a workplace thrive. Disregarding these expectations and treating people as disposable is setting the workplace up for failure.

Long-term success cannot come from such short-term strategies that use people up and promptly let them loose. Having a human touch in the office means real engagement, communication, and being able to feel secure in our roles.

It used to be that a job was just a job. Letting someone go meant very little because you could always find someone else. This is still how some businesses operate, especially in food and beverage and retail.

However, times are changing.

Companies are expected to have a social conscience–they are expected to be aware of climate change, racial inequality, and additional important movements. When a company continually makes a showcase of dismissing people out of flagrant negligence, the public will see this and act accordingly. It is in the best interest of the company to support its employees in a manner similar to their clients.

Respecting your employees will bring clients to your door time and time again. It will also improve working relationships in the workplace. This will encourage your employees to be committed to a company that cares, and committed to their roles.

The best sort of employee is going to work in a position where they are appreciated, taken seriously, and treated respectfully. If you want those types of professionals, then you need to create that type of atmosphere in your workplace.

Establish the Right Priorities

A company exists to serve its clients and customers. However, there is no company without employees;

if you circulate your teams through a revolving door, then there is no solid foundation for the long-term success of your organization. The focus in the workplace should be on meeting expectations and accomplishing goals. Every role will have unique priorities to focus on. Beneath it all, it should be built on a foundation of expectations that are outlined in the company's mission and goals.

Leaders can prioritize the bottom line all they want but losing sight of the people who are making that happen will only create problems. Employees will leave and your reputation will suffer, preventing you from replacing those employees.

While every professional needs to focus on their responsibilities, it is vital for leadership and HR to not lose sight of their people. This includes prioritizing not just the results that they bring to the table, but their current status and daily task load to see how well they are functioning.

Answer these questions for yourself to see how well you are supporting your teams:

1. **How are you supporting your employees in their daily tasks and career growth?**
2. **How are you helping them to develop their skill sets to improve their output?**
3. **How are you engaging them to ensure that they are satisfied in their jobs so that they stick around?**

Professionals like the chance to prove their worth and their independence. As people begin to work from home and remotely more often, it presents the possibility that they know what they are doing and do not need any assistance. Maybe they do not need assistance, but they do need support. Every professional needs it, whether they know this or not.

The human touch helps professionals to use their humanity to connect with other people.

In order to continue growing in their profession, your people should have someone working with them on a regular basis (weekly and quarterly, dependent on time and agreement) to grow. This requires those in charge to make time and prioritize their subordinates and team.

Prioritize your people in their development, their growth, and their regular contributions to the company.

This does not mean treating them to lunch every day or hovering over their shoulders. When you prioritize your employees, this means that you are making sure they are well-equipped to accomplish their tasks, you are answering all the questions they might have, and you are prepared to support them when they tell you that a problem has arisen.

By giving your employees time, equipment,

training, communication, and the knowledge you have, they will know they are being supported. It gives them the awareness that you trust them to do their job. You can let people work independently while still prioritizing them in your daily responsibilities. It is not that people need a hand to hold–they simply need to know that they will not be left alone whether they fail or succeed.

When they are treated as an afterthought or as disposable, morale and productivity are guaranteed to suffer. But when people are prioritized and are given all that they need to succeed, they will thrive along with your company's bottom line.

Establish your people as priorities from the very beginning.

The time for using employees up until they have nothing left to offer is no longer the way we run businesses. Instead, we now must prioritize the internal development and growth within our companies; it is the surest way to bring in new clients, retain current clients, and continue establishing the brand within your industry.

By putting your people first, you will have a whole team to back you in turning the focus over to the client. You need to trust your people and support them so that they can do the same for you and the company. The act of prioritizing people in the company is an important responsibility assigned to both leadership and HR. Through your example, your coworkers will know how to put people first. Succeeding in a profession requires the support of the people around you.

A professional like yourself should always be dedicated to ethically and responsibly achieving the mission set out before you to accomplish. As this is done, you must keep in mind for yourself and your employees that there is a difference between loyalty and commitment.

Why Loyalty is a Risk

Everyone speaks of customer loyalty to ensure satisfied clients always return. There is less spoken of employee loyalty in comparison to employer loyalty, even company loyalty. Many high-level executives like the idea of their employees being fully tied into the brand--even when it is ultimately not in anyone's best interest.

Rather than expecting an employee to be loyal, invite and expect them to be committed.

Telling employees that they must be loyal to your company removes their freedom from pursuing what is best for themselves. It detracts them from investing in their future, requiring them to sacrifice part of themselves and their attention.

By asking an employee to be committed, you are changing the culture for Millennials. This is very important to note as you hire the younger generation, even Gen Z as well. Professionals will switch jobs when they can to find a better place.

Do not ask for loyalty. Your service and products should be able to speak for themselves. Ask for commitment, that no matter how long they are with you they are committed to your mission, values, products, and team.

Having a team committed to your company speaks loud and clear to others outside of the brand. The world will take notice and more clients will come your way.

A lot of good internally and externally will come from taking this route. By encouraging commitment over loyalty, you are showing the employee you value their personal growth.

Commitment is a character trait, and this behavior is taught through life experiences and decisions. By learning about your team's habits and experience, you can learn quickly to see who is able and willing to commit themselves to the cause of the company.

If you are seeking to become more aware of their behavior, offer this while discussing soft skills. Are you hiring people who can commit themselves to a mutual goal or cause bigger than themselves?

This will be important to take note during the hiring process as well as with employees already established in the company. People change and our skill sets do, too. If someone has commitment issues in the major areas of their personal lives, they are not going to be able to properly commit to you as their employer.

During the selection process, you can look at the accomplishments of an individual, as well as their job history, to see about their commitment strategy.

Ask yourself: based on their answers during selection, have they shown a commitment to school or an organization in the past?

Change your expectations about your future employees. Push loyalty out the window in favor of a more useful and promising attribute. While loyalty and commitment sound similar, the way they exemplify themselves in the workforce will be different.

Expect your people to be committed to your organization while they are employed at your company whether that is six months or six years. Consider the type of effort that will be made.

Company loyalty does not guarantee hard work.

A committed employee will have an honest view of the company where they understand improvement can take place and will be actively engaged in doing their very best work. This also ensures self-awareness. Not every employee is meant to stay at the same company for their entire career. Committed professionals will know when it is time for them to leave so they do not hinder the company's growth. Knowing they cannot do anything more, they will make room for those who can.

I would rather have an employee who is 100% committed for one year than an employee who is 50% committed for five years.

There are several reasons why an employee may not be able to commit at the beginning of their career and why that might change. It can stem from their personal lives, current worldly issues, or situations at work.

New management can conflict with personalities, making your employees lose focus and their desire to do well. Once respect is lost, it is hard to regain. Employees might lose commitment through depression, projects they struggle to understand or make progress with, and if they lose funding. New employees might have accepted the job out of desperation and necessity without ever having really wanted the job. Experienced employees might see the changes coming their way as a sign that they are no longer equipped for their jobs.

As you can see, there are countless examples of why employees may struggle to become or stay committed in their roles.

HR and leaders cannot fix every issue. There will always be struggles. But it is possible to build up a company culture with processes, benefits, and systems that will fulfill the basic needs of all employees. Then, when there are problems that do arise, you can work with those struggling employees to see if this is the best workplace for them to be.

Even if you lose a few of your employees during this, you will find that others will grow more committed because you have showcased your strengths. A company requires hard skills and soft skills to make progress.

No one is exempt from the need for commitment in their roles.

Life tends to be one version of 'Follow the Leader' no matter how old we are. Employees will follow the examples of management. If the company has certain rules that those above them are not following, then employees are less likely to follow those rules as well.

Everyone must keep their commitment, including leadership.

If an organization wants employees to be committed, then the organization must be committed to its employees. If the organization says they are committed to sharing a training program, they must provide a training program.

Employees want to know they are valued and the best way to exemplify that is for the organization to keep its word. Commitment is a lead-by-example type of behavior. A company has its values in place for a reason; it is for its employees as well as its customers. If leaders are committed to the mission, values, and qualities of an organization, the employees will follow suit.

Commitment Works

Cultivating commitment to your organization starts at the very beginning of the application process. When an organization is honest and transparent with its candidates and employees, they build trust without leaving room for surprises.

People want to feel secure, and when trust is broken there will be a lot of insecurity. This leaves a shaky foundation for anyone left standing when things take a turn for the worst.

In the workforce, a candidate or employee will decide to switch companies and employers if they feel insecure about a job. When a candidate starts a new job, sometimes they have just taken a leap of faith to do so. So, when they get in a position that is not what was advertised, they feel lied to and insecure, resulting in low productivity and turnover.

Fortunately, there is another option: being truthful. These are just a few of the perks to honesty and transparency in the workplace: secure employees, low turnover, higher productivity.

This is not just beneficial for the company's workplace. It will translate outward as well. The company's reputation will skyrocket when word gets around that they are an honest and trustworthy place of employment. Which means more qualified employees and more customers, which then equals a bigger increase to the bottom line.

If a company is committed to its employees, the employees will in turn be committed to their company; they know the company has their back and that will make employees proud to work for the organization.

Commitment does not have to end during the termination or resignation process.

Some companies go as far as throwing going away parties or celebrating the employee's departure. This action shows the immense character of an organization; when I look at these celebrations, I see commitment.

An organization celebrating the commitment of an employee shows they value employees no matter how long they stay.

The downside to these celebrations is consistency.

Is the company going to continue them for everyone regardless of how or why they are leaving (not including disciplinary)? Are the parties going to be for all resignations even some that were mutual?

The upside to these celebrations is that it allows the organization to showcase its commitment to its employee's growth as individuals. These displays of commitment may allow and encourage current employees to feel more committed to the organization as it displays its commitment for them.

In this process, it is reasonable to expect a certain level of commitment from your employees.

Reasonable Expectations

We have discussed in detail how much salaries and benefits can impact a workplace. As we review the desire and the need for commitment from employees, we need to be realistic about the expectations that are set upon everyone.

Everyone deserves to be paid a living wage. Salaries are necessary so that people can afford to survive and support the economy. But this is rarely the most important value that employees are looking for.

They want particular benefits. Sometimes these benefits will come in hard or technical forms of health insurance and other times they will appear in soft forms like fulfillment.

It is human nature for people to want to make a difference in the world around us. We often consider ourselves to be part of something bigger than ourselves and we want that to matter. Having a position at a company where they can make a positive impact is sometimes more important than the paycheck they take home. This is one of the reasons that people take on jobs in social work and at non-profits. They want to be in a position where they can help others lead better lives.

Fulfillment is a powerful aphrodisiac in the professional world whether you realize it or not.

You can pay someone double their expected salary and offer them benefits only to have them refuse the job if it is not something they are comfortable doing in their career. This can go against their beliefs, their desires, their family values, or something similar that may be equally important to them.

We need to respect everyone and their values. Ultimately, you would not want to bring someone onto the team if this is not where they want to work.

There should be room for opportunities in the workplace for professionals to seek out fulfillment. Whether this is in community service projects with their team, creating earth-friendly products, or being able to do the work that they are passionate about, leaders and HR can reach out and find ways to help their employees.

Whether they do or do not, that is not up to you. What is up to you is creating those opportunities. Not only will doing so benefit you, but it will positively affect the entire company. Doing this can also present your brand in a positive light to your customers.

It may be difficult in the beginning but that does not make it impossible. Connect with your coworkers to see what they desire in their lives and how they would like to make an impact.

One of the best ways to get started in doing this is by reviewing your core values and principles at the company.

These may change with the times. No matter what they are, it is important that you maintain those standards and use them to the best of your abilities to better the workplace. This will encourage your coworkers to be consistently focused and committed to their responsibilities.

Company Values Exemplified

Establishing and supporting company values sets a precedent for everyone to follow in their work and relationships in the office. Every company must have its own values prepared by the leaders and HR with a well-rounded understanding of the company's history, purpose, and future.

One of the core tenets I have prioritized and have seen most effective in the companies I consult with, is *transparency*.

Inclusive of truth and honesty, transparency in the workplace is keeping your coworkers aware and updated of changes in the business and policies with an open door to communication and answering questions.

Let your employees know the state of the business, whether good or bad. This gives them the knowledge that they may need to push themselves and their teams to do more. Let them know that bad things happen to you as well, showing that you are human and relatable.

To only see one side of people sets an unfair and unequal expectation. You can educate your employees with the goings-on of the business while maintaining high standards of behavior and work ethic. It can be something this small that makes your employees more committed.

Even as some employees leave, willingly or not, this will stick with the employees who remain. People who understand and have the same values are bound to work better together.

If you do not have company values established, now is the time to get to work. If you do have them, take the time to review them with your team on a regular basis. Hold yourselves and each other accountable by always doing your best. These values should be reviewed by everyone in the workplace regularly--no one should be exempt.

Establishing company values will invite more participation, hard work, and commitment.

Use your values to encourage commitment so that you can grow alongside your employees. People will come and go but you want them committed while they are with you.

HR is *Sexy*

Forward Motions

Commitment can go a long way in improving workflow, employee morale, and progress in the workplace. The focus on employee loyalty needs to go. When you tell your teams that they have to be loyal, this removes their freedom from pursuing what is best for them as an individual. Focus on commitment instead, creating a more healthy and transparent culture for employees of all ages.

Step One: Talk to Long-Term Employees

Through surveys, questionnaires, or conversations, talk to your employees.

There is a reason why some employees have stayed so long with your company. That would include anyone who has been there for over five years. This is your opportunity to reach out to them and ask what has prompted them to do so. You can do this through a variety of methods to see what works best for everyone included. Ask them about their expectations, concerns, favorite benefits, and what has inspired them to stay in the same workplace.

Step Two: Connect with Struggling Employees

Seek out your employees who may be lacking initiative or desire to succeed.

This can be done once you have gathered your data from the first step, or it can be done at the same time. There are people struggling in your workplace while others are thriving. Reasons may vary from personal or professional issues. Seek them out and talk to them through any preferred method. This conversation will be more sensitive, so make sure everything remains focused on the workplace. Ask them about their struggles and whether they have a plan to encourage themselves to start improving soon. If one person is struggling, more people might be struggling as well. This will help you gather better insights on any potential problems at work so you can start creating solutions.

Step Three: Talk to Long-Term Employees

Develop three to five changes in the workplace that can be implemented to support your teams.

As you work through the first two steps, you

should be gathering data and finding holes in the workplace relationship that need patching. You have listened to your coworkers. Now is the time for you to build a strategy of three changes that can create a positive impact for the company. Whether you can do this yourself or need support from other leaders, use your data to see where the gaps in employee satisfaction are to create lasting changes.

As you listen to your employees and begin to establish these changes, you will find that work will get a little easier for you and your teams. When people are heard, they will reciprocate in kind. Your coworkers want to be able to do their job. When you create the right atmosphere, they will be able to do their best.

Employees work harder for companies that they care about. By setting these expectations, you are bound to have a thriving and successful workplace. Company values like transparency and honesty will make all the difference in improving commitment in your workplace.

Part 3

Your Employees

Chapter Eight

When I started my business, I remember the thrill of taking on my first big client. I arrived at their place of business so that I could start working with their teams. I was training this large corporation to use a learning management system (LMS) and helping to organize their branding and messaging in training.

Excited, I looked around and was impressed with their offices. I arrived and stayed in the front, patiently waiting for my escort while I wondered what it would be like to work with so many great people. I had heard great things about this company and their teams; I felt as though I would fit right in with them.

My escort needed to walk me through the HR department in order to reach the conference room. I was excited for this because I love HR and was hoping I would be coordinating with some great professionals there.

They were sectioned off and nestled away from everyone else at the company. This caught me off guard, along with how no one tried to speak to me. Everyone just stood to stare and whisper.

I could have thought, *"Oh no, are they talking about me?"*

Instead, my gut reaction was, *"I hope they treat employees better than they treat their visitors."*

Over the next three days, I interacted with many employees, always returning to the HR department where I was helping them with their training strategies. This gave me time to carefully listen and watch how this team integrated with other employees. It was only three days, but it quickly depressed me. Before it was time for me to leave, I could already tell who would be walking out the door if I were leading this department.

●

Claims that I do not know what was going on behind the scenes or could not understand all the work on their plates are not strong enough in this situation. I know the HR role and how well people can manage such a position. I understand more than anyone the excuses you can make for not wanting to communicate outside of your HR world. It is not enough. You must be better than that and your employees deserve better.

As I have said before, HR is not just a job where you detach yourself at the end of the day and go on your way. Our jobs require physical, mental, and emotional effort to make it through the day. Be careful who you listen to when people are suggesting a job to you. There is a chance that you will excel, but there is always a chance that you might not. This includes paying close attention to how well you do in certain situations.

We can often think that we are good at one particular skill that will help us excel in the job, but sometimes that is not enough, and we end up making ourselves more miserable down the road.

The field of human resources is particularly complicated. Your job is to help support the people within the entire company, not just one team. It is an in-between sort of role that is often messy with a heavy and complicated workload.

Many people think they would do well because they enjoy working with people. But it is more complicated than that.

As you can see from my story, you can like those you directly work with but not care to interact with others. HR staff who treat their internal team members and guests as secondary will ultimately fail their organization.

There is no true success at work if you cannot share it with those around you.

I had arrived in high hopes and the expectation

to at least be spoken to by those I met upon my arrival. I was there to support them in their work like they support the employees of the company. Though I attempted to converse with several people, no one returned the favor. It happened to other employees who attempted to communicate with their department as well. The HR department did not care to engage voluntarily with anyone outside of their team if it could be helped.

This is why company culture matters. I went into the office like anyone else might have in having heard great things about the company and being excited to work there. It made sense to me that if they had good reviews and a nice office that they would be friendly and engaging. But this was not the case.

Everyone outside the company should have a good idea about the true company culture through the appearance they give off. If these are not synced, then they are, in essence, lying to the outside world.

The culture is meant to be set up in advance before the company grows big with employees and customers. It needs to be created, established, and maintained. HR and leadership have an obligation to support this and need to hold one another accountable.

This is beneficial for countless reasons. Employee engagement, employee retention, better customer relationships, and even improving the bottom line. A company culture established expectations regarding policies and procedure, while holding people accountable who violate these rules. Employees can be treated in a respectful manner with one another, better manage conflict resolution, and address uncomfortable situations.

HR should play a vital role in strengthening the workplace to deal with these occasions. With leadership, they should be holding each other accountable for conversations and situations that do not meet the company culture standards.

Establishing the Company Culture

We have talked about the company culture and need to iterate just how important this is. People often come and go for this reason.

Every company's culture will decide how leadership treats their subordinates, how teams work together, and ultimately sets the mood for every part of the company.

Leaders and HR need to establish one whole culture or employees will create several.

Company culture will exist in a workplace no matter what. It can either be purposely intended or accidentally created. People will come together in forming their own groups and decide on matters as they go.

A company can hope that it will all work out well. Or they can take matters into their own hands and control the future possibilities about company culture. Everything with a company should be managed so it is not left to chance. If HR and leadership does not make change, the employees will create their own cultures.

This is not necessarily a problem, not at first. Departments with different focuses and responsibilities should have a culture that is their own. But what happens when they start to contradict or become problematic?

We have to be prepared for anything that goes wrong. And that means having the groundwork for company culture already established. With set values established, everyone will know where to start and grow from there. This helps everyone work toward the same goals in the company no matter their actual role or responsibilities. Employees thrive when they have clear direction. It is also important that HR and leaders have this clear direction so they know how to lead, support, and address sensitive situations in the workplace.

Establishing a company culture is vital for ensuring everyone is prioritizing the right values and handling their tasks and workplace relationships in a focused and respectful manner. Once it is created, the culture needs to be continuously maintained so it continues to create a positive effect in your workplace.

Guiding the Culture

The last chapter focused greatly on the importance and benefits of transparency within a company. Whether you consider this a key attribute in your company or not, it is vital to at least use it when it comes to the company culture.

Through guidance and continual effort, you can maintain a culture that positively impacts everyone with whom the company interacts with. Employees, customers, and clients can all see your company in a positive light when you do this right in a continual manner. This means that what people know and see about your company on the outside before interacting with you should remain the same once they have interacted with you.

I should not have a preconceived notion of your company based on branding, reviews, and media that differ from what I find when I walk through those doors and begin interacting with your employees.

You and your teams need to represent the company well. When this does not happen, it tends to occur because there is a lack of communication, camaraderie, and effort in workplace relationships.

Leaders and HR are meant to set an example in ethical professionalism in their roles. When employees do not see this, then they will not take action and do the same. That is why the establishment and guidance of a culture has to start with HR and leadership.

Employees will take note of this on their very first day on the job. They will see how HR treats new hires, their department, and speaks of others on their team. As they are onboarded, they will see how their leaders act within their department and outside of it with other employees. They will study what behaviors are expected, how people act, and the reactions they garner.

Humans naturally want to fit in. If the employee deems this a workplace where they want to stay, then they will aim to become like their coworkers.

The best way to guide a company is to let everyone know the direction where you want to go and how to get there. This transparency will help your employees to feel secure, lower your turnover rate, and increase your productivity. Your company's reputation can skyrocket when word gets around about your honesty and trustworthiness. More customers mean a bigger profit and more success. It can become a positive circle of growth for everyone involved.

This goes back to commitment as well. How can a company guide their teams if neither party is interested in furthering any long-term goals?

If a company is committed to its employees, the employees will in turn be committed to the company. They will know the company has their back and that will make employees proud to work for the organization. Leaders need to build those goals, and HR can build the strategies to create cohesion and employee support.

Transparency will take you a long way as a company. In order to show this by company-oriented values and by example, ensure that everyone is well versed and educated in clear communication.

Being able to clearly communicate is especially important in guiding the company culture along.

Because we are adults, we often take information and ideas for granted with the idea that we do not verbally have to explain ourselves. However, communication is not that simple. And to prevent mistakes from happening, it is far better to over communicate than the opposite.

This is a skill taken for granted as we are taught our native languages and pick up industry lingo as we go. Real communication is more than just responding to statements and questions. Communication is about listening, understanding, and moving a conversation along. From my professional experience, everyone could use some time dedicated to working on their communication with others.

While it is easy enough to train people in communication, one needs to keep in mind that it requires other soft skills to succeed. Patience and empathy are very important when it comes to communicating with one another.

It is also important to take into consideration that people are raised in different locations and cultures with family and friends who play a big role in determining how we all come to communicate. This can produce a variety of results; some of them will work out well and some of them will not.

For myself, I tend to communicate in an honest and frank manner, preferring to get straight to the point instead of beating around the bush. I do not believe in fluffing up conversation because I have heard too many people who take one sentence and turn it into an entire book.

This way of working has not always worked well in the workplace. That is why we need to constantly be learning and improving ourselves.

Once, there was a leader who recommended that I soften my edges when talking with other people. A few situations had occurred that jeopardized workflows and relationships, so he talked to me about the points I could correct and where to improve. With honest feedback and his support, I have been able to find that middle ground where I can be both honest and respectful at the same time.

This leader guided me with a focus on transparency so I could understand what was happening and used supportive communication to help me gradually learn how to improve my skills in the workplace.

Guidance is best supported one-on-one and it can work its way through the ranks in your company to make sure everyone receives the support that they deserve.

Both HR and leadership is necessary in guiding the company culture along. Leadership needs to take an active role in establishing working relationships that will help build the culture as they go. It is up to HR to ensure that everything is moving along in a cohesive manner. Take charge of the culture so that you can guide it in the right direction.

Responsibility of HR and Leadership

It cannot be forgotten that you are in charge of affecting real change in your workplace.

This is a message I have to state time and time again to my clients. No one likes hearing about the responsibilities they have put on the backburner.

HR is *Sexy*

But we cannot talk about company culture without discussing who is responsible for it.

Without a hands-on approach by leadership and HR, your company culture will be spotty and aimless, filled with flaws and potential contention. The only way to build something positive and promising for your team is to purposefully create it.

The sooner you can accept your responsibilities and act in accordance with them, the better off your teams and company will be.

Actively taking action will help your culture to thrive. It will produce opportunities, opening windows that had not been there before.

This means consistently putting in effort to the company culture. Without it, the culture will grow stagnant, and employees will begin to stray in their commitment. A company culture needs to be created at the founding of a company and revisited regularly to see if any principles or values need to change.

The better you know your culture, the better you will be able to help your current employees and hire the right people as you grow.

Both HR and leadership will bring important perspectives to the table as you reflect on how the company culture has evolved and evaluate how to move forward. You can take the pieces that are working and expand on important aspects, making it a focal point to train, coach, and reinforce the new culture.

Whether your organization is in its early stages, or already matured, culture change is reinforced when employees witness leadership engaging in these culture-based behaviors.

If it needs to be changed, it will always be possible. A company can make an external rebranding for their customers and can do an internal rebranding for their employees.

The first step to changing culture is to discover what the organization needs to change. This needs to be pinpointed exactly in your review. Consider the HR processes, leadership procedures, and employee engagement in your efforts to locate any particular problems.

You can ask questions such as:

1. **Do your leaders face repeated resistance to procedures or rules?**
2. **Do your employees have common fears within the organization?**
3. **Is there a common thread of situations that HR must deal with regularly?**

When you seek answers, you may find more than you could have expected. It may not be easy, and it cannot be done in an afternoon. This will take time and it requires leadership taking an active role in discussions with employees, as well as with HR to get at the organization's current culture.

After ideas and solutions are brainstormed as a team, HR's role is to research best practices to determine if there has been any information provided by other organizations who had the same issues. That data can be shared with leadership as you review company culture and how to proceed forward. Together, armed with data and new strategies, leadership and HR can solidify a preferred solution and an execution plan.

Own your responsibility. Use your soft skills to remain patient and flexible when reviewing the company culture. This will affect your rules, decision-making processes, and how you handle your employees.

They are the people who you need to concentrate on when you are building the company culture. Consider realistically how your decisions will affect them. Put precautions in place to protect your employees where they need protection and where they need to use their own responsibility. These people deserve a chance to thrive as well as a chance to be aware of what is going on in the business around them.

If you want your employees to celebrate and enjoy

the company's success, then they should also be there to address and accept business struggles. The more people know, the more they are equipped to help.

HR especially must pay attention during this time. As a human resources representative, you are responsible for the *people* aspect within the company.

At the beginning of this chapter, I discussed how the HR team I worked with for a short time was unfriendly to visitors as well as those in other departments. My biggest issue with this particular HR department, besides being inattentive to the employees, was how they thought they were untouchable. They operated under the assumption that they were 100% secure in their role.

When the HR department is focused on following only the expectations and desires of leadership, they are not shy from reminding their employees that everyone is expendable. At the end of the day, we are all replaceable.

So, as you focus on your company culture, make sure you are focused on the right goals and are not wasting your time or anyone else's. When you feel as though you know everything and there is no need for development or change, then it may be time to turn the efforts to someone better equipped for such a responsibility.

Problems in Workplace Culture

No matter how hard you work or how much you may care, there will always be problems in the workplace. Sometimes there is something you can do and sometimes it is out of your hands. The bigger a company is, the more that professionals like to blame the employees.

However, problems tend to be conflicts within a company culture and exacerbated by those in positions of power.

We all know that power corrupts. I have watched many people in management positions lie and because I did not have the facts in writing, they were able to continue doing it.

My favorite mentor once told me it always catches up with them. At the law firm I worked at, there came the time my leader was replaced and the new one who came in would try to do things that would make me and the rest of the team like her. She tried to befriend us with compliments and cheerful chatter.

However, I noticed in leadership meetings she would lie. Her facts would be wrong though I knew she knew the correct numbers, and she would make false claims about the team. I was not sure if anyone else on our team was catching it, so I kept it to myself.

Then one day in a meeting, the COO asked if I had worked on a particular spreadsheet that he sent over. My boss said she had sent it to me and that she had not gotten back from me. This was a lie and put me on the spot with our executives. I did not know what else to do but shake my head no because I had no idea what she was talking about.

I looked at my computer and that is when I received the email from her with the spreadsheet. Though I could tell them that I had the information now, I was unprepared and left stranded in the room with my coworkers.

Eventually, the meeting ended. My team went straight to the COO right afterward to tell him what my leader had done to me.

I did not talk to my leader for fear of being gaslit or ignored. About a month later, I was laid off. This hurt me deeply and has stood as a prominent reminder to me that we can only do our best and there is no controlling what comes next. Never be afraid to lose your job for doing what is right.

Leaders like this one would have reasons for their actions, even though they would not be good ones. People tend to act out of shame and fear. This can reflect poorly in their management styles and within the company.

A company that is failing does not want people to know they are failing, whether they are failing financially or culturally. This is where a lack of transparency exists, creating problems along the way. Those in power often believe that it is easier to keep people in the dark, never confirming or denying the rumors. No matter a person's position, they are still prone to facing fear and doubt in the workplace. If companies are failing financially, they do not want their employees jumping ship.

While these feelings are understandable, the actions these leaders take are often not reasonable. Bringing transparency to the front as a key principle in the company can be difficult and complicated at times.

Leaders need to be willing to brave that step. And when these situations come along, HR should be the guide in these areas bridging this gap. Being able to communicate important information so that it does not incite fear or embarrassment but truthfully gets the message is a vital skill that needs to be used to support employees in every level.

Sometimes, leaders forget how they got where they are now. Once in an ivory tower, it becomes harder to climb down. It is as though because you can see outside it, that you can see well enough. But often the situation is that you are not close enough to understand what is going on down below you. Without a true and cohesive understanding, there is little that you can really do.

As you excel in your career, it is easy to be forgetful about who gave you a chance and helped you along the way. People also forget how they felt the last time someone treated them badly, so they do not always realize what they are doing.

HR has a duty to point this out to them along the way. The more HR is willing to speak up and address problems as they arise, the more change that can be made. It is about reminding them that showing how relatable they are with their staff propels the business, it does not stall it.

We have also discussed what it is like in dealing with problems with the employees. They outnumber leadership and have their own emotions and ideas in mind. Sometimes someone just is not a good fit at a certain company, whether this is realized during or after the hiring process.

The company culture can face all sorts of problems, ones that you can prepare for along the way. You can establish work environments that are productive, collaborative, and innovative so that they do not have as many issues.

This will help you to hire the right people and even deal with the few employees who may not be following the mission and values in a fastidious manner. There is a way to do everything right in the office, just like it is possible to do something wrong in the workplace.

Doing It Right

Even if you have not seen an excellent company culture in your own career at this point, it does not mean that it is impossible to achieve.

I have worked with plentiful clients who have done many things right as well as those who have made mistakes along the way. Often it tends to be a mix of the two, where dedication and optimism for change is finally put into play with the necessary time and money to do so.

One of my clients stands out.

Their company has been in operation for over one hundred years. Their staff is experienced and well-tenured; many of their professionals have been there for twenty, thirty, or even forty years. In this era, that is both rare and incredibly impressive.

I had the pleasure of connecting with many of these professionals. As I talked with them, I discovered that these employees were extremely loyal and dedicated to their work and the company. Many have and will end up retiring after having worked with this company as their only employer. How many companies today can make such a claim?

This has impacted the way I support my clients and help them to achieve the same, if that is what they are looking to do. Companies today can only dream about having leaders who truly know how the company operates inside and out, employees who are dedicated to the company's mission and values, and overall low turnover. The commitment from these professionals is amazing.

And they have a reason for it.

We already talked about how commitment can make such a difference in your company. It is one of the ways you can create that ideal company culture and do it right for your employees.

Oftentimes, culture is the one thing that people talk about most when they are leaving the office at the end of the day. They want to gossip, discuss the problems they face with company rules, and complain about their disagreements with coworkers more than review the details of their projects at hand.

People are more emotionally driven than we would like to admit. The company culture will get discussed by your employees with strangers, customers and clients, and friends. These people will gain a new perspective about your company and will most likely share the stories they hear with those around them.

Consider how this may affect your bottom line. It can go uphill or downhill from there. Fortunately, there is something that can be done. You can take control of the narrative by establishing a strong company culture that protects, supports, and benefits your people.

Strive for employee commitment because your coworkers are a company's best sales team.

While you cannot prevent every employee from ever saying anything negative about their time at the company, you can take the time to be proactive in creating a space where they can enjoy their time at the office.

When you create the right company culture, you have the potential of bringing in more customers and increasing employee engagement. This especially helps those team members who interact with clients. Happy employees are most likely to provide excellent customer service.

Just because you have a late start on establishing or improving the company culture, does not mean that it is too late to begin. It is always better late than never. Pick up your feet and get to work to create a better atmosphere for those working at your company. In order to improve your company appearance, concentrate your efforts on the culture between the employees.

There is no single or particular way on how to create the right culture.

This can be difficult as well as a boon in your

endeavors. The groundwork you build off on should include transparency and communication.

People need to be made aware of the important things in their office. Everything else should be set up to support the employees, no matter their position. The directions and goals need to be supported within the culture. It will take time and attention, but it is worth it. Creating the right company culture can ultimately decide whether your business continues to survive.

Forward Motions

It is tempting to use the excuse that we cannot control people and, thus, cannot control the company culture. This is creating a false narrative that will only lead to difficulties down the line for you and your people. We like to consider that appearance is superficial, but you will have many potential clients who take you at face value. The best way to present that perfect image is to create what you are looking for in the first place.

Step One: Discuss Transparency Insights

Learn from your employees about transparency concerns and improvement.

The best way to ever learn about a problem in a company is to talk to the staff and employees about the situations they face on a regular basis. You can talk to your employees at various levels to see where the gaps of knowledge are and to see what they are missing. The more people you talk to, the more you are likely to learn about the transparency at your company and how you can improve it.

Step Two: Explore Culture Opportunities

Meet with HR and leadership to consider where updates can be made.

Start talking with those who can make changes. Work with leadership at the top and make your way down to see how the current strategies might be affecting the overall company. There may be patterns that you have not seen before this point. This gives you a chance to do something about it, to work with HR and leadership to consider new strategies for the workplace culture.

Step Three: Review Onboarding Process

Find the gaps in the hiring system to provide potential recruits with transparency.

Internal strategies and plans always need to make an appearance in the onboarding process for new employees. These people will be trained differently than those before them. Reviewing the gaps of knowledge in the hiring process is helpful both to current team members and those just starting out at the company. No one should have to work in the dark without knowing where they are going. You can review the current processes for onboarding to make sure everyone is being set up for success in their new roles.

Everyone is accountable for their actions in participating in a company culture. Whether you are conscious of it or not, you are either helping or hindering it at any given time. By taking these forward motions, you can now act purposefully and see the impact that you create.

People tend to create and commit to their first impressions within just a couple of seconds. You have an opportunity in your position to do something about it--for your clients and your employees. Create a positive professional appearance for your brand by creating the right company culture.

Chapter Nine

I spent years working with others and working for others in the human resources field. This allowed me countless opportunities to work with all types of people and leaders while showing me that I did not want to work for someone else.

There is a difference between taking on clients and having a boss. I could choose one and not particularly the other. When I worked for a company, I had to follow their rules, meet their expectations, and sometimes do things that I did not believe were best for the company or for my employees.

Because of this, I decided to build my own company.

My previous employer did not want me to go, but this is what I wanted. It was important to me to build up a company where I could make a positive impact in my own business as well as those around me.

Building my own company gave me the opportunity to start something from the ground up. I was able to establish a foundation dedicated to reshaping our business world with dignity. With this purpose in mind, I spent a lot of time cultivating a strategy on how to best help my team start in the right direction and work towards the same goals.

This took time, attention, and dedication. It surprised me that this was a continual effort that I needed to update frequently, discuss with my team, and establish new policies that were unique compared to most I had faced by that point in my career. Creating my company taught me how it is possible to direct your people in one centric direction through strategy and effort.

Your team needs to work in the same direction with the same goals.

These are not the same thing. Having a direction is like having a compass that you use to guide you along the way. This can be inclusive of the industry you are in, your purpose, and your goals. The goals are the specific milestone(s) you make as you progress.

Goals should be created in line with your direction. If they are not in sync with one another, then you will pull your team down the wrong path and you will not be able to move forward together. A disjointed company cannot hope to stand on its own feet when this happens. The inevitable pulling and breaking will occur, potentially creating a permanent fracture or worse.

You owe it to yourself as well as your company to make sure that this does not happen.

Start solving this situation before it becomes a real problem. Build your team up in a manner that will ensure continued success even when someone important leaves or when the industry begins to change.

Learning to place importance on soft skills in my offices made all the difference. We focused on building up wisdom, honesty, and integrity among ourselves when we first started out. With these skills of ours, we began to work together as a team to encourage these values while we were in the office. And then we started applying them when we were with our clients. It was amazing to see the positive impact it had in our partnerships and how it improved our work on a regular basis.

These skills are not dependent on culture, age, race, or in any other structure by which we use to define ourselves. Anyone could develop and use these types of soft skills wherever they might be and in any profession.

Hard skills are necessary for a job, but soft skills are vital for a career.

To ensure your success, you need to help your company to succeed. That can only happen when you work alongside your teams and bridge the gaps. The better you are able to do that, the more likely you are to have all of your people--including your customers and clients--succeed together.

It comes back to having that same direction and those goals that help you achieve this.

Collective Vision

Cohesion is the act of creating a united front or whole. You need that at your company for your people to focus. A collective purpose in a company can be simple or it can be vast. The most important thing is that it must exist.

There will be slight variations, that is obvious.

And yet they are still all part of the large picture. Small teams might have focused goals regarding their unique projects with deadlines for separate clients. Research and development departments will have different goals from those in the marketing departments. These differences make everyone and their roles unique and important.

But collectively, their goal is to support the company.

All the small goals that separated people and teams and departments will still need to come together to have a higher purpose of helping their company achieve their mission in a specific manner synced to their core values.

Having a focused goal to work toward is not just beneficial for the company's continuation, but also helpful for your employees.

People crave purpose in their lives. We want everything we do to have meaning. Jobs used to be simple roles where they came and went without feeling too committed. That has since changed over the years as we consider our careers to be part of who we are, part of our identity. Whether it is providing excellent customer service or creating new technology, we like the idea of our work to mean something.

Do this for your employees. You can show them the importance of the company and the positive effects that it provides in the lives of your clients. By giving them a chance to better understand the purpose of their work, the more eager they will be to do it better.

This is what we could consider a *soft benefit* because it is not tangible and it may not even be lasting. As we discussed in earlier chapters about helping your employees to become committed to the company, offering different types of benefits can help prompt them to stay longer on your team.

A salary is only one benefit and not always enough. Healthcare and retirement support is also expected.

One other thing they will greatly appreciate is

being able to work in an environment where they are positively impacting the world around them. You can give your coworkers a great cause to work for that is embedded in your company culture and that encourages everyone to support and strengthen each other.

I have learned during my career about the various ways this can be brought about. From start-ups to older companies, from various industries and cultures, I have learned the main steps necessary to bring about that collective vision at every company.

Communicate Your Goals

If you want anything done at work, it needs to be said.

Written down, emailed, messaged, verbally-- however you like to communicate, it needs to be clearly done with your teams in order for anyone to know what you want. Expecting people to read your mind is impossible.

This is a problem that I have encountered one too many times in the workplace. Leaders have so much going on in their minds and on their plates that they never take the time to consider that they have not actually talked to their teams in detail about the work that is supposed to be happening. As for HR, they have a knack for expecting everyone to understand exactly what they mean without explanation regarding compliance documentation, HR lingo, and other communication misunderstandings.

We are all bound to make mistakes along the way. What we need to be able to do is own it and learn about what is not working.

As our society continues to become more technologically driven, our methods of communication will keep on changing. Email, the first electronic messaging capability, is even going out of style with other programs for instant messaging or video communication.

Though you may have a preferred form of communication, it does not mean that your employees will be guaranteed to use it. You may need to compromise or adjust your communications strategies to connect properly with your people.

When you are able to funnel communication in the right way to get your points across with your people, then you can make sure to get the right message to them.

A standard form of communication needs to be instituted. This will ensure everyone in the company can hear it one way or another, in whichever manner is best suited to succeed. Only once you have that prepared can you start to share your goals.

Now that you have a bridge of communication instituted in your place of business, you can start to share your message. This needs to be done in a clear manner, succinct if possible, while using words that are understandable and can be recalled at a later time.

Consider how we create branding and sales pitches to the public. A confusing message that rambles on will not be remembered which means that your team will not be able to keep that centric focus. Your message needs to be memorable if you want any action to be taken. Clear language can keep you from bogging down your ideas with too many distractions.

In sharing your message, it will also give you an opportunity to set reasonable expectations.

Be sure to present the expectations you have for your company and your teams within achievable standards. There are those that you are meant to achieve in your role, those that the company is meant to reach, and those for your people to meet.

I gave my company, and thus my team, a direction to work in where we work to help other professionals support their own teams. It requires daily effort to work in this manner. With that direction in mind, I instituted goals to help us make progress along the way. All of this had to be communicated in a way that was easy to comprehend and thus capable of accomplishing by my team.

When you can connect with your team in a way

that they can listen to you, this gives you a chance to exchange knowledge and work together in the same direction.

Implement Your Strategies

Creating a plan can often become overwhelming fairly quickly. With so much on your plate to handle, with people to listen to and support, we find it difficult to implement new strategies in the workplace.

Leaders and HR will have different ways to proceed in this process, just as it will vary per goal that you are working toward. Achieving goals can become intimidating which will make it harder to get started. By taking it one step at a time, then you are more likely to succeed. Now that you have communicated with your teams, it is time to get started.

My work is focused on helping companies to improve their HR team and strategies in a way that will support employee retention and make room for new ideas. I follow a simple and proven method for getting started.

The first step I take is reviewing their compliance issues. With the team, I take the time to connect with them where we address the simple matters first. This allows me to see where they are and where they can improve. It requires me to put in easy work to ask certain questions that could include:

1. Do they have I-9s filled out correctly?
2. Do they fall under EEO-1 reporting?
3. Are time and labor processes both adequate and efficient?
4. Do they have a process for missed punches?

You have to take the time to cover the basics so that you do not risk missing simple concerns later on. This allows you the chance to review their current processes and how that has worked for them up to this point.

Afterward, I proceed to review that FLSA requirements are being met with positions, job descriptions, etc. This allows me another glimpse to see how well they follow through with the law and take care of their team members. It starts to create a well-rounded picture of the team's working style.

Following compliance, I dive into my client's handbooks and policies.

This gives me a chance to see their best practices and the values they have put upon themselves and their employees. It shows me if they meet federal and state guidelines and helps me to learn if they are applying these matters appropriately and consistently across the board.

I finally finish my review by talking to the employees to gather their insights. This is added to my wealth of research and review so that I can start taking action. What I do next depends entirely on what I have learned up to this point.

In this same manner, I built my company and now support clients in a like manner. I do my research and then take action. HR needs to be able to handle issues like this. As for leadership, they need to be made aware of projects or similar matters that may affect their role.

You may follow a similar type of procedure. Otherwise, you can establish your own. It should be a process that you can repeat when necessary, following guidelines that you know to be important.

The most important step is to simply begin.

Too many of my clients like to do their research, study their options, and then take a break.

Usually, this break does not have an end date. Without getting started, the same problems will continue to arise. They may begin to fester and cause permanent damage along the way. If you really want to help your company, you need to be prepared to act.

We like to think that nudging people to move in the right direction is easy, that people want to work together. This is not always the case. It is also a bigger problem when people do not completely understand the situation before them. There is the chance that you will need to return to communicating with your employees in order to ensure they truly understand.

Only once everyone is on the same page can you implement your strategies. This is not the time to leave people in the dust. Everyone in your place of business has a right to know the direction that the company is taking as well as the right to learn about the goals that they are supposed to be working toward.

Implementing your strategies that will support these goals does not need to be a chore. It is a perfect opportunity for you to connect with your team as this process begins. Make room for questions and concerns along the way. The more people you bring in to support this process, the more people will understand and be prepared to help their team members to succeed.

Progress does not come by accident, which is why we have to hold ourselves and each other accountable for all that we do.

Accountability

If you want initiative and movement in the workplace, then you need accountability.

This goes for you as well as your team members. Accountability is more than just showing up every day to sit at a desk. It is about ownership, follow through, and a high level of reliability.

You can showcase this in proactive communication by asking those questions and searching out those answers. When you hold yourself accountable, communication becomes a key part in proving your commitment and your focus. Most things need to be said and expressed within the workplace instead of silent expectations or hopes. When we are looking to hold ourselves accountable or want to hold someone else accountable for their work, then this needs to be said out loud.

There are projects, meetings, and a hundred other small things in the office that request our time and attention. We always have a lot to do. But this is not reason enough to slack off and leave your team to handle everything.

We cannot control all that happens around us. However, that does not mean that we are incapable of doing anything. This is often seen as being reactive to certain situations as they arise. It is like accepting accountability for something that has already happened and perhaps has gone wrong. But we need to be proactive as well.

It does not have to be intimidating or terrifying. We accept accountability for our errors as well as our achievements. No matter the end result, nothing is permanent. Mistakes happen and we have to understand that. Anyone who expects perfection is going to be sorely disappointed. When you accept accountability for your work, you are given an opportunity to grow.

Without accountability, there are miscommunications and delays. One person's mistake will eventually trip everyone else up. By not taking responsibility for your actions, you are risking a lot more than it is worth to hide something. Problem upon problem can arise in this situation to eventually make everything fall apart. Holding yourself accountable is very important and will most likely separate you from those too afraid to do so.

When you do take ownership of your actions and consequences, this shows that you are more emotionally mature than the majority of the workplace. This gives you a chance to set an example to make your office a place of growth, innovation, and progress.

Flexibility

Structure is necessary for a company's maintenance for continual work and process flow. Professionals need guidelines and an organization needs to be organized. There are rules to follow, compliance to follow through with, and a list of requirements for everyone working. In the middle of all this structure, a particular level of flexibility is necessary.

This plays perfectly into the need for allowing dignity in the office. There are always exceptions within a certain situation. Between the rules and requirements, leaders need to be flexible so they can assist and adapt to their employees' needs.

Companies need that human touch to balance flexibility and rigidity.

Many leaders make unnecessary decisions for their teams by adding rules and complicated structures when they are afraid of losing control. Leading is a difficult responsibility, but it does not bode well to add too much onto the plates of other employees. Team members have enough on their plates.

However, there might come a situation where structure is needed because of those taking advantage of generous flexibility in the workplace.

All benefits and blessings can be taken advantage of by those who want to use the system for themselves. If the offer of flexible hours, duties, etc., is no longer benefiting both parties, then it means it is no longer doing any good.

Flexible working locations have been growing in popularity over the last few years as more professionals begin to work from home. This can be due to health, distance, and many other reasons. Work production has gone up during the majority of these occasions.

Yet once in a while, there are employees who take advantage by posting false work logs and falling behind on their responsibilities.

Benefits are provided with an expectation from both parties. If one continues to give without a return, then it is not fair to the other party. Employees have a responsibility to their leaders just like leaders and HR has a responsibility to them in return.

An organization should lay out a consistent plan for how they handle flexibility, whether it is by policy or documentation. This needs to be collaborated on with HR and leadership. While the C-Suite should have a say in the matter, they should not be the deciding factor when they do not work with the majority of their employees who will be needing such benefits.

Then the strategy for flexibility needs to remain consistent, maintained within all levels of leadership. It should be handled the same for everyone. No exceptions, even for C-Suite.

There may be times when a single mother has been given every opportunity to be on time, including moving her schedule and helping her find childcare. You have done what you can but she cannot make it to work at a reasonable time. In HR, your duty is to the company as well as the other employees. To enable continual tardiness and disrespect in the office after providing every opportunity available is a dangerous risk.

Other employees and leadership will take note of this, learning to resent the organization and create issues within the company culture. Certain employees cannot be held to different standards.

There can be structure within flexibility. Together, they can help create a supportive and winning hiring culture.

Emotional Intelligence

One of the key attributes of holding oneself accountable for their actions is having emotional intelligence. We discuss this in the Introduction in regard to emotional maturity and how it may be the most important soft skill that a professional can access while working.

When we accept a job offer, we are accepting accountability for a certain role that comes with requirements and expectations. This means that we have responsibilities that are meant to be handled and a direction to work in.

Emotional intelligence will help your coworkers to better grasp the focus for the company and manage the goals.

There needs to be balance in handling your emotions while on the job.

This important skill is not becoming more *popular*, but the awareness of its name and necessity in the workplace has grown substantially in the last twenty years. When people use their emotional intelligence in the office, they better understand what others are saying and are more likely to use their soft skills to thrive.

While emotional intelligence may not come naturally, it is a skill that can be worked at with continued dedication and effort. Starting out by listening and empathizing with others is a good beginning.

HR especially needs to be well-versed in this if they want to be able to bring that human touch to work with them. We need to be able to find a balance in supporting the company and advocating for our employees. Taking someone's word on everything is not the right way; rather, it is by listening to several people and taking into consideration the big picture.

With the ability to manage the company culture, HR needs to hold themselves responsible for supporting diversity and inclusion. That is a key goal for human resources in general, and needs to be able to correlate to the direction that your company is moving in.

This is where leadership needs to step in alongside HR, encouraging the growth of emotional intelligence with their teams. It is also vital for leadership to be self-aware as well, ensuring they do not allow favoritism, nepotism, or other similar mistakes.

When a leader ignores emotional intelligence, then they are more likely to lose good employees who have a wealth of knowledge and talent to share. The good team members will leave the company, leaving only weak links. We have exemplified what it means to be a good leader throughout the chapters, and one of the key attributes to ensuring a leader's success is with emotional intelligence. Leaders are responsible for setting their teams in sight of the company's direction and they need to be able to do it correctly.

As HR and leadership cultivate emotional intelligence in themselves, this will set an important example for other team members. Those who have it will use it, and those who do not have it will begin to learn about it.

Employees do not always feel comfortable putting their skills to use in an unhealthy work environment. You can help your teams thrive by creating the right setup for your people. This can lead to improved work performance, better communication, and meeting goals that have been set to guide everyone toward the company's direction.

Emotional intelligence is a great benefit for all professionals. In order to stay focused on the company's direction, employees need to understand, be able to communicate their concerns, and work together.

Supporting Employee Behavior

No matter a person's hard or soft skills, the way they are used and developed are all controlled by the means of human behavior.

Philosophy and psychiatry are still aiming to understand what creates a person with their soul and their mind. Everyone has their own ideas and beliefs about who we are and whether our future is predicated upon some other basis of knowledge.

This will encourage coworkers to do the same.

I know well that addressing one's attitude in the workplace can be problematic and sensitive. From the time we are children to the time we are grown up working at our jobs, there will always be adults telling us that we can or cannot talk about one thing or another. It can be difficult to find the right setting for a conversation as well as the right words to say what is necessary.

There was no place in the business world for talk about finances, politics, religion, or any type of workplace harassment. We have ideas that are not allowed and words that cannot be said while on the clock. Some professionals want to restrict even more subjects and there are others who believe that nothing should be considered off-limits.

At the root of the matter is a person's behavior. The way that they present themselves, the ideas they share, and their reactions to the world around them.

People make mistakes and their behavior is not always going to be respectful, understanding, or easily managed. HR is tasked with the expectation of being able to understand and handle situations when they arise, no matter how their coworkers are behaving. This can include the leadership as well, making their own mistakes.

While HR is there to handle the crises, it seems that people are beginning to expect their employers to pick up where parents and school left off in their education. When it comes to work-related training, that is true. A company should always be cultivating a wealth of knowledge within its employees. Professionals are hired with the expectation of their ability to communicate, listen, and work well with their coworkers.

This may not always be the case, which is why an investment into soft skills for an employer is necessary. While they may have coworkers who struggle to listen and collaborate with one another, that does not always mean that they should be let go.

This is where the balance between hard and soft skills comes in. When one outweighs the other, the company can take the time to invest in the development of correcting and establishing a standard of workplace behavior.

Even now, there are thousands of companies who willingly put up with brilliant and hard-working employees because their skill set is so vital, even when their behavior may be problematic. A company should not have to compromise with harmful attitudes just to succeed. That is not a promising move, exemplifying what they are willing to put up with so long as their team has talents.

Most employees learn their work behavior from prior places of employment and prior employees they have worked with.

Consider the children's game, "Monkey See, Monkey Do." We become like those we spend the majority of our time around. If we spend forty hours a week in the office with coworkers, we are bound to become more like them.

Employees will mimic behavior that others do because "they get away with it" or "it works for them," but with a new employer, it will not work at all. In the workplace, we have a responsibility to set a good example to our fellow coworkers on how to work for our companies. Human Resources plays an integral role in building and launching training to continually develop an employee's workplace behavior. These trainings must be specific to your workplace and the needs of the business as well.

As you create opportunities for your team members to cultivate their skills, make sure that you are not leaving anyone behind who could use a lesson or two.

Professionals need to learn hard skills and soft skills. You can create the right opportunities to build the best team possible with the people you already have by giving them the time and tools they need in order to thrive. When you do this, your team will grow in skill, ability, and become committed to the company.

Only when you treat your employees right will they be able to properly do the same for you in return. It is a toxic relationship when you do not support them in this manner. And when this happens, you will lose the commitment of the employees who you are getting rid of as well as those who stay behind and keep their jobs.

Commitment to your employees can take you a long way. It is time that you shift your paradigm from loyalty to commitment, inviting your coworkers to stay through your ethics and values during their time of employment.

Never set unreasonable expectations because it will only cause damage in the long run for the company, which is exactly what you want to avoid.

Without One Direction

Guiding a team of professionals in one direction can be easier than herding cats when you do it right. But there are missteps and situations that can arise, causing people to start moving in different directions.

This can take place in the company culture with divisive workplace practices, unprofessional mannerisms, and a lack of communication in inter-department workflows. I have seen this in my past work experiences as well as with my clients today.

My first HR position was a struggle and an important learning lesson. While I loved what I was doing, this position made me question whether I even wanted to stay in HR. The leadership would just bow down to those at the top of the company.

When employees feel that no one understands them or is working on their behalf, they immediately become defensive, hard to work with, unhappy, and most importantly unproductive. The workplace was already complex at a local prison and adding contentious leadership did not help the situation. When you work in a prison, the dress code is really important. Dressing inappropriately, especially as a woman, can cause disruption to the prisoners and the staff. It can create hostile environments, workplace harassment, and even sexual abuse.

Solutions to improve a situation can come from people in any position, those who are ready to make the path easier so everyone can move in the right direction.

Over the years, prisons found that employees that did not dress in uniform were better off in the workplace by wearing overly modest clothing. You needed to wear sleeves to cover your shoulders and wear longer skirts, for example. This was beneficial for limiting workplace incidents in a large capacity.

And then suddenly, corporate changed the dress code at their level and then rolled it down to the facilities.

Women were no longer required to wear panty hose or sleeves, just to name a few of the restrictions lifted. This is not a concern in the majority of workplaces and could have turned out very well. But in our work at the prisons, it opened the door for one too many problems. I could not understand why this leadership would make a decision that could very easily cause trouble. A dress code was not focused on ensuring everyone looked like a professional, but that everyone might be safe in the workplace.

I asked bluntly, "Have any of you in corporate ever worked in a prison? Do you realize the can of worms you just opened?"

My disagreement with this decision was the beginning of the end for me there. I had the proof to back up my concerns and legitimate reasoning to explain myself, but they were not interested. Not long after this incident--propelling more trouble along the way--they began talking about moving me into another position where I would not be able to use my voice to raise my objections and concerns.

This went on and was exacerbated with the incident where Jake was not told of his termination before their disciplinary hearing. I did my best to support this employee who eventually went on to fight for and win his job back along with his certification. Every situation where my leadership saw me as a meddler and troublemaker is where I was committed to helping our employees to better manage their jobs.

We all thought that we were moving in the right direction. But without clear communication and structure, it was obvious that our ideas were not in sync with one another. They focused on the company and how they could succeed even if it caused damage to their employees. They wanted to look better than how they functioned. The vision they were looking at was much different from mine.

Without everyone working in the same direction, we were moving away from one another. Problems were bound to arise and eventually resulted in my leaving the company.

Professionals have a responsibility to do their best in their workplace. But in order for us to do that, we need to create an environment where this is possible. That will not happen if the direction of the company is not clear, and the goals are not lined up accordingly. And when you are finally able to bring about clarity, you can start to make real and long-lasting progress.

Streamlined Progress

Whenever you are starting a new project, you need to know how success will be defined. For example, friendship is about having someone you can connect with and turn to when you need support. A school project is about learning what you have been taught in class and being able to showcase your knowledge. Your company will have a similar concept of what it means to succeed. Through products and services and experiences, the point of your work is to help the company to satisfy customers in a particular manner.

Some of the goals that you set at your company, either for single teams or everyone, can be accomplished in literal terms with proof.

There will be other goals that are not so easy to distinguish in this manner. But just because they are more complicated does not mean that they cannot be worked towards. When your company is making real progress, you will know it.

Nobody succeeds by accident.

Success is the result of a deliberate effort made within a team. Your employees will understand their responsibilities and expectations. HR will know how to support the goals that are set as leadership ensures they are managing the right atmosphere and projects to help the company thrive.

As everyone focuses their attention and energy on the correct and singular direction of the company, the goals will fall into place to make strides in your workplace efforts.

Working together with that mentality may be the change that you have needed this entire time. Your teams can be organized so much so that they are able to accomplish task after task and project after project. With everything in its proper place, your progress will become streamlined so that you succeed time and time again.

To do this, you have to put in continual effort to get the results that you are looking for.

When it comes to working with people, we need

to know the right time to redirect our projects or start afresh to stay focused on the end goal. It is easy to give up when we are frustrated, and it is even easier to lay out the blame upon others when things go wrong.

Quit playing the blame game. When you focus on what went wrong, you will always find that it goes back to a disconnect with your people and the company's direction. That will show a gap in the process that you can fix so that it does not happen again. And then you do your best to keep moving forward. Systems are fallible and we need to always be vigilant in keeping an eye out for catching problems before they cause real and lasting damage.

As you fill in the gaps and correct flawed processes, this will give you the chance to see what sort of progress your teams are capable of making. Leadership will have the responsibility of guiding them along the way while HR, the ideal HR, is supporting every team member at the company.

Forward Motions

You can guide your company by establishing a direction to always be working in. As you proceed forward, setting goals that run parallel to these efforts may be paramount to your success. Get started on this process by following the steps below to become more aware of everyone's understanding of the company now and how it can improve.

Step One: Make a List of Expectations About Your Subordinates

Review job requirements and company overview for employee engagement.

This is your chance to review what your team is bringing to the table currently and where they could be doing more in their roles. List out the responsibilities that they are required to have, the skills they bring to the table, and any gaps that they might have in between. The better you understand where your team members are at professionally, the better you will be able to see how well they are connected to the long-term goals and direction of the company.

Step Two: Make a List of Expectations About Your Superiors

Discover Leadership Requirements and Responsibilities for Direction.

Professionals tend to do the same sort of work every day in the terms of working on certain projects in a certain manner, talking to the same type of people, and so on. Whether you connect with your leader or study the example they set, you can take your time to consider the expectations of your leaders in the workplace. See which expectations your leaders focus on and see how well that is meeting up with the company's direction. This is not meant to judge anyone for their workstyle, but as always, it is an opportunity to learn why people do what they do. If you do not have a leader, then explore the leaders within your company. And then you can move on to Step Three.

Step Three: Make a List of What Your Company Expects From You

Note down your job requirements and any recent goals made with leaders or HR.

Just like you did not judge those in Steps One and Two, you are also going to avoid judging yourself in this situation. Instead, you are meant to see how well your actions and skills play into your role in regard to how they benefit the bottom line at your company. This is your chance to reflect on not just how well you are doing and how you can grow, but how you can use this as a chance to ensure you are moving in the right direction with the purpose of the company.

The three steps listed above are all very similar to one another. While many of these steps do appear simple, it is important that each of them is taken seriously. By observing company requirements and employee responsibilities, you can learn a lot about how the brand presents itself and whether that is effectively helping everyone to work together.

Everything we do is essentially required to have a certain level of effort. You can spend as much time on this project as you like, similar to all of the other steps in this book. Accomplish this however you desire-- just as long as you are also taking into consideration any progress being made alongside the potential for creating a healthy workplace. And with that, comes the need for an ideal HR.

Chapter Ten

The question will have to be asked at your company, when do I know that we have reached that point where our HR department is ideal?

Just like tests are graded to show you what went right and wrong, you can do the same in your departments in the workplace. Certain standards will need to have been met in order to achieve a passing and exemplary grade. Most HR departments are barely passing. Consider these as the achievements you must meet in order to find yourself with an ideal HR department.

- Happier people, meaning improved retention rates in a place where teams enjoy working together in the office and connecting away from their desks. This means HR has the chance to ensure compliance and employee satisfaction, bringing employees together in a variety of ways. With more people coming in instead of out, you will be able to see the positive impact going forth within your company.

HR is *Sexy*

- Improved business, meaning that your company's reputation is positive and your partners and customers are eager to connect with you. This means that HR is helping the company to practice good customer service while also helping to project safe, honest, and ethical practices. As you pick up more business, you will find that when everything runs smoothly with the team internally, it helps the company to run smoothly externally.

- Gross earnings, meaning that revenue is growing. It may be gradual at first or it may skyrocket, but there will be more money along the way. This means that HR is hiring the right people who can excel in their role and produce sales and positive interactions with clients and customers. More money is bound to come in when the business and employees are thriving.

With these three markers passed, it means that an alignment has been achieved. The only way to achieve all three of those concepts is to ensure cohesion between your people along with the company's mission, vision, and values.

Getting to this point requires effort on the part of everyone at the company. Employees need to be focused on their job and trusting HR. Leadership needs to be focused on the company's direction with established goals. And HR needs to be permitted to work alongside that leadership in building such goals to support the employees and the company. We all have a job to do and projects to complete. When we do things right and put in the necessary effort, then we will have the chance to succeed together.

Some will say that it is not worth their time or financial investment to establish strategies that promote employee engagement and improve workflows.

I would argue that you cannot afford to miss out on such a valuable opportunity. The good things in life often require more effort than we expect to give. But you will have had a chance to see through the past chapters that your investment can be repaid tenfold when it is done right.

When you give your company the attention it deserves, it will return the favor.

Everyone Needs the Ideal HR

Most companies slough off when it comes to the HR department. Even the experts within the field do not care like they should. It is considered dull, full of paperwork, and useless. They spin it for themselves and others in a way that detracts from its value, claiming it could never be sexy.

If you are just doing the bare minimum, what can

you expect? Effort is rewarded in all that we do when it comes to preparing meals, starting relationships, and building up the HR department. You can make the department an engaging and exciting place for comfort and growth when you change your outlook and begin to cultivate a sexier workplace.

Human Resources is the heart of an organization.

That should be attractive enough on this fact alone. It has capabilities and a reach that other departments in the company lack. HR has a profound impact on the entire business and having an inadequate HR staff--or no HR--can severely damage the efficiency and production of your company.

By not ever giving it a fair chance, how can it ever prove its capabilities?

This is why we need this revolution.

With the realities of the multigenerational workforce, it is imperative that HR becomes a strategic partner with your leadership team as to, not only retain top talent, but to ensure your company is an ideal place to work.

A well-functioning HR department should be a partner to your leadership team to equip them with the tools and confidence they need to properly address business issues. The department is the main place within a company that produces a culture of internal business owners. These owners, these leaders, should and must want success externally and internally for the company. The only way to ensure that is to be certain everyone works well together.

HR should not be the enemy of your leadership team. Rather than always saying "No," HR should arm leadership with options.

These options allow your leaders to own the decision-making process and the outcomes of their decisions. Employees should have faith in your HR department. They need to know that anything sent to HR will be resolved promptly and appropriately. These actions prevent feelings of disregard and neglect. Both employees and your leadership team should recognize HR as an advocate looking out for their best interests.

While HR supports employees, it should also be a bridge that connects all parts of your

organization.

Once this connected and cohesive atmosphere is achieved, your organization will be more successful. This means that your HR will have gone from bleeding money to actually adding profit to your bottom line.

No matter the cause or mission of your company, the organization must make money to survive. This means the basics are necessary to have established-- most of which encompasses compliance of local and federal law along with having people who can work well together.

We have discussed the need for having the basic groundwork done and a foundation firmly put into place. This cannot be reiterated enough because of how important it is; even a tiny fracture can bring a building tumbling down. The same can happen to your organization.

So let us consider the people who help prepare those building blocks.

Most seasoned business owners today are those who belong to the Baby Boomer generation back when a professional clocked in, put your head down, did the work, and clocked back out. This generation typically had very limited personal interactions and understandings of their workforce.

The evolution of the workplace has provided these owners with the opportunity to know their workers and learn more efficient ways to work.

We have the younger generations flooding the workplace, taking their role in society. These are the generations who have been raised on technology and now crave that human-to-human contact. They crave this so much that they even look for it from their employers.

There are perks and concerns that can be noted within anyone who uses their age as an excuse about their lack of growth with no desire to learn. This affects both leaders, middlemen, and HR. Employees who work for standoffish leadership may struggle to succeed as they often feel undervalued.

We talk so much about the human touch because of how relevant and necessary it is for things to function in a company like yours.

Everyone watching their back means they cannot look forward.

Most people would rather point fingers than solve a problem. Too often there is a lack of accountability in the workplace. No one wants to make a single mistake, so the blame game will be tossed around instead of searching for real solutions. Every problem can have an answer. But if one person on a team is unwilling to do their fair share, then nothing will get done.

People put themselves on opposite islands, prioritizing themselves over the company. I have seen this happen too often to let it slide by any longer. Companies want to cut through the red tape and I want to cut through the ego. Holding onto pride will not do good for anyone in a situation where problems are starting to happen.

One issue will arise and then another, quickly putting everything and everyone in danger.

We can pretend this does not happen, risking the chance that we will get carried away with the problem sooner rather than later. If we do not wish to do that, then we have to be ready to open our eyes to the reality of our situation. Only then can we start finding remedies to solve these problems and get rid of the danger.

If you really want to find a solution, then you will dive deeper into the situations at hand. This will help you to better discover how you can utilize your team and skills to solve the problems as they can. As you become more aware, you will understand the root of the dangers at hand, along with whether you need assistance.

Community Inside the Office

We like to sell a dream in America that we work because of our passion and should only take jobs that support such a notion. This has grown through a history where people have been able to make a living in all sorts of ways. One would think that with time, there are more possibilities. In some ways, this is true. Yet for many people, it is not.

The people at your company may not be there because they love the company or the work. They will sell themselves in the interview and they will work hard, but this is not their passion. Do not discount them. This is done so they might have a living.

How much do you think that general workplace mistreatment affects the cultural dynamic of a community?

It is *incredibly* detrimental. If the community is small and there are not a lot of places to work, employees are pretty much forced to work at the same place to pay their bills. Without a lot of options, they will do what it takes to survive and keep bringing in whatever money they can for their homes and families.

Employees are then forced to endure workplace mistreatment to survive. This should never happen in any situation, and you have a responsibility to stop it when it comes. If they ever get a chance to leave, they will. But you should never put someone in such a situation where they must deal with any type of harassment or misconduct.

When someone complains but does not quit, it means they are asking you for help. They are asking for change. It is up to you to help them. When you improve the situations for your employees, the community outside of the company will do better.

I speak business talk to owners but not with HR. When my owners come to me, they are tired. Tired of red tape, of not being able to do anything and not knowing what to do. I am there to stop sugar-coating the matter and to bring up alternatives that have not been seen as an option at that point.

This allows me a chance to remind owners and leaders that they have a responsibility to support their teams beyond just financially. A company is not a family, for they are more similar to a small community. Not only does everyone work toward improving their collective situation with a goal to work toward, but they learn to rely on one another in many ways.

All types of communities run into the occasional problem.

I have had clients who have spent months arguing with the prior HR staff. In one case, the owner wanted to move some salaried employees to hourly, because they felt the team deserved overtime.

Their HR representative told the owner that this could not be done because it would be violating the FLSA (Fair Labor and Standard Act) rules. While the HR person was not wrong (especially if the job description is not modified and they are still completing tasks assigned to a salaried role), they were not able to do a good job in explaining the situation to the owner.

Moving an employee from salary to hourly is actually benefiting the employee, whereas if it was the other way around, it would be benefiting the employer and could potentially cause some issues. That was when I stepped in. My alternative to the owner was to restructure their departments, recreate job descriptions that are more in line with the hourly role, and move those employees.

At the end of the day, it made everyone happy, and the company was still in compliance.

Building up that community will become much easier when you have your company's mission, vision, and values aligned and communicated across the board. This will improve team progress and revenue along the way. Besides, the more you do as a company with your teams, the more opportunities that will come your way.

As you bring your people together and build strategies that support your company's goals as well as your teams, success will come to you.

You can showcase your capabilities through conversation, philanthropy, and honesty to keep growing. Conversation is about building that connection, casual or formal, and molding it into some form of a relationship. Philanthropy allows you to focus on causes that your company cares about or those that your clients are involved in caring about. As for honesty, it is important to always be truthful to your teams and your clients.

These can quickly become strengths that will allow you to showcase the best aspects of your company for those who matter most. It bridges the gap between leadership and employees for cohesion and progression.

Leadership and Employees

I believe it is important that employers stay patient and flexible during tough times, like the COVID-19 pandemic. I know it is hard because employers have been hit just as hard as their employees. Often when one thinks that everything is about to get easier, it only grows more difficult.

The best thing leadership can do to help their employees succeed in the workplace is to listen to their teams.

Employers need to listen and be more active in what is going on in their employee's world. Whether it is a single parent struggling with school closures, a grandfather who has underlying medical conditions that is afraid to work in the office, or a single person trying to navigate doing 3 people's jobs because others are out sick, you need to be paying attention.

We had a client who would supply breakfast and lunch for their employees, so the teams did not have to worry about using their own food during work hours. This client has also extended lunch hours for parents who had kids at home, allowing for more flexible work hours so long as the employee was able to get their work done.

Recently, one of our clients suspended their PTO limits and thus allowed their employees to use time as they needed without worrying that they will not have enough time to cover the unexpected during a pandemic.

These changes can have a drastic impact for a business. When an employee knows that the company cares, they will return the favor and work their hardest for the company.

Listen to your people and you will see what can be done to help them.

How can you make decisions across the board when you have no idea how it may affect one department to the other? Leaders must understand the workplace and what their employee's jobs are. Meet your people where they are and then you can move ahead together. Of course, this will not fix every problem.

Difficulties may still arise. Will you always please everyone? No, because that is not possible. But if you make a fully educated decision, and your employees know that you did your best, the buy-in is so much easier.

This will put your team on your side as you look

to create that great company and the ideal HR. After all, you need your employees to be thriving for HR to show they are doing their best.

Moving Forward

As you create your HR department and turn it into the ideal setup for your organization, the opportunity to keep moving forward is available to you.

HR must come out of their office and away from the desks to be a part of the organization. Just doing this can make the company blossom and grow. This is a perfect opportunity to evolve into a business partner and build with the business as a professional or team of professionals.

After all, consider the lasting impact of the department. HR is solely responsible for the employee experience from recruiting to termination. Ensuring training is adequate to the company means going beyond creating a cookie cutter mold to work with. Every situation is unique and bumps in the road will always be there, no matter how far you have progressed. Stepping up allows you to ensure that leaders are driving the wheel with their employees, and not just HR. Being fair and consistent regardless of who writes their paycheck.

When we grow, we are benefitting ourselves and our organizations.

Building others has given me training and hands-on experience in leading others. With this knowledge, I have been able to secure more leadership roles within other organizations. It helped to provide more experience for me that I have been able to apply everywhere else. Training should be viewed as networking, whether it is within your own organization or another organization. In the past, I have had leaders that would give me more tasks and more responsibility based on the new skills that I acquired through training others.

Human Resources is focused on improving human relationships in the workplace.

In the big picture, HR stays constantly connected to leadership.

How can leaders promote relationships with HR? As a CEO of an HR company and realizing my clients all discounted HR, I had to wonder how I could help build trust among those teams? I believe HR needs to show leadership that they present solutions and options. Once this is done, a leader can spearhead the inclusion of HR to be seen as a valuable part of the team. A CEO must use HR and show the team how well they work together. The buy-in must be a prioritized goal in the HR department.

HR is more than just a job or a career. It is an opportunity for professionals to work together to

HR is Sexy

create something more than themselves. We can and need to move past the days where they are spies for leadership and only seen as a hindrance in every role.

An HR representative can affect important and vital change at an organization. Taking these steps will help us all to break through those stereotypes to bring about great benefits for your company.

Making progress is not always about taking huge leaps; instead, it is often accomplished by taking baby steps in the right direction. You have done this by way of my "Forward Motions" throughout this book. They have helped you to consider your role, your organization, and the flaws and potential improvements that are possible.

Congratulations on making it this far. Now, you are ready to show that HR really is sexy. I look forward to seeing how you can revolutionize your company.

Forward Motions

Establishing the ideal HR is possible so long as you are willing to put in the continual effort that is required for maintenance. Action must still be taken when you climb a mountain, whether you continue your way upward or begin your descent. Creating a healthy and professional environment for your HR team will create a transparent office that is capable of properly supporting other team members and the company. As you take these forward motions, you will be able to reflect on the progress you have made and all that you are able to do moving forward.

Step One: Review Your Progress

Pull out your "Forward Motion" lists to compare the progress and work.

You have made it through to the end of this book, allowing you several opportunities to work through these action steps. Now is the time to bring out your papers and to compare them. You can see what work has taken place, that which still needs to happen, along with any personal modifications that you may have not noticed before. Review your progress and see how far you have come.

Step Two: Create a List Pertaining to the Ideal HR

Establish what the ideal HR looks like at your company.

The ideal HR will not look the same as it might appear at your last company or at others. It may even change at the same organization over time. These are necessary changes and should not be discounted when making progress. Progress is, after all, change. Create and refine that list that is necessary to creating the ideal HR. Then you can begin to create a strategy for your brand and install the right program for you and your people

Step Three: Bring Your List and Plan to Your Team

Strategize with your department on how you will establish the ideal HR.

The time for waiting is gone. You must take action to create the ideal department at your company. You have had chapters to explore the type of necessary leadership, how to better support your employees, and the steps you need to take in order to establish progress. You can pull your notes together and work with HR and leadership at your organization to create the right kind of change. You have had a lot of time to research and consider your ideas, and now you can begin to implement everything you have been wanting to do for your company.

You have read this book and have been reminded that the world of Human Resources is filled with potential. It is sexy, everchanging, and meant to support employees in the professional world.

These "Forward Motions" have closed each chapter with the purpose to provide you opportunities to reflect on your knowledge and make changes for lasting improvement in your workplace. Whether you do them all or a few, in order or not, what happens next is up to you. It is important to note that a person can be given all the advice and instructions, and yet accomplish nothing. This is your opportunity to create change.

Conclusion

Starting on the Human Resources track was the hardest thing I could have ever done, while simultaneously the best.

It has taken me years of blood, sweat, and tears to reach where I am now. Supporting businesses and professionals has allowed me to grow personally and build up a thriving company.

There is no glory in Human Resources. You do not join this industry for the attention or awards or the pay. You do it because you care and understand that everyone deserves to have a voice in the workplace.

Yet even when the chips are down and everything is going wrong, there is the beautiful aspect of HR that makes it sexy. It is a position of adventurous problem-solving and speaking up for those who don't yet have their voice. HR is sexy in its capacity to build employee engagement, ensure compliance, and support leadership.

This has taken me years to understand, however, and I know that people struggle to understand it now.

This is a challenging field. There are days where we will feel trapped and lost, uncertain of how to move forward.

Years ago, I once said, "There has to be a way to make HR better."

I made the statement out of frustration as the Human Resources world continued to fail me and those I worked with at the time. Nothing seemed to be going right at the time, no matter what creative solutions I came up with or problems we moved past. While I believed that HR was created for everyone's benefit, I could not accept that this was how it would always be.

It is possible to move beyond the regimented systems of the past and the rigid plans in favor of something better. With the right flexible systems and a personal approach, any HR professional or team can help a company hire and retain its employees while also ensuring a healthy and friendly environment. This is something that I have dedicated myself to learning and developing for myself, my companies, and my clients.

Such dedication requires time and effort from everyone involved. I have gone through the difficult work myself to establish a paradigm shift so I can focus my attention on where I can do the most good. In HR, I have built a career for myself focused on helping others.

It is because I love HR and my career so much that I know it needs to be better; it is not reaching its full potential and it is up to people like us to make lasting improvements. This is why I am not afraid to point out what needs to be mended.

When we love something, we have to do our best to help it heal.

I have seen the flaws and failures of HR management first-hand. This is why I say that the world of HR is currently broken. Not permanently, and perhaps not even within every organization, but it is broken to the point of needing to go through a thorough healing process.

We cannot give up just because something is hard. There were roadblocks after roadblocks for me along the way. Like other HR professionals, I encountered countless flawed systems and leaders who enforced programs and strategies that were not there to improve employee performance.

When I took an early HR job in the retail industry, my store manager told me that part of my job was to follow the employees--our coworkers--around to keep an eye open for dress code violations. I felt like I was spying on my team when I could have used that time to create a healthier and friendlier workplace.

That is not what I had signed up for!

For a department with the word "human" in the title, we were damn far from providing that personal touch. There have been countless times when I felt as though I was drowning under those rigid procedures. And right next to me, the people in my department were just robots parroting meaningless words from our distanced and distracted C-Suite.

It was during that time that the only *fun* or *creativity* permitted in my roles meant planning workplace parties. There were birthdays, holidays, and retirements that were opportunities for everyone to enjoy. That was not exactly the lasting impact that I was looking to make for my team.

I knew there was still a lot that needed to be done to improve the employee space in every company I was a part of, so I kept my eyes open and looked for a chance to make some changes.

Create The Change

Since I have always marched to the beat of my own drum, I started doing things differently.

My strong, no-nonsense personality was done allowing the flaws and breaks to remain in my workplace at the time. I began pushing back. I started holding everyone accountable and doing away with senseless drama. I made managers have conversations with their subordinates and watched difficult situations unravel peaceably when everyone came together.

I will not say that this happened quickly and that every problem was soon fixed perfectly with everyone happy. It is not how that works.

There were difficult moments where certain choices had to be made but I always held my ground. When I invite change into a comfortable setting in the workplace, I know that I risk being ignored, demoted, or even fired. Not everyone wants to hear what I have to say. That is something that I accept and even welcome if necessary. Men and women throughout history have done what they believed was necessary no matter the consequences. I believe that I owe it to them as well as you to continue such a journey.

Though difficult and occasionally impossible, I have never given up on this revolution.

It was a struggle to educate professionals on the shifting mindsets and flexible programs that needed to be put together to ensure everyone's satisfaction. Everyone wants to believe that they have the best ideas and that through their personal beliefs and strategies, they can mend every situation. But they are incorrect.

If you want your ship to sail, you must all be sailing in the same direction.

HR is *Sexy*

We all have ideas and many of them are great. But only a few of them will be useful or wise for the workplace. Sometimes the effort we put in is well-intended but misdirected. It was clear to me how lines were continually crossed and how miscommunication increased.

So I worked hard to bring everyone together to work in the right direction. The more I created new strategies and updated old procedures, the more I began to see how my ideas could positively impact the organization.

My parting words to you are to say thank you, to share my gratitude for making it through this entire book. It has been a learning experience for me, taking years of practice and failure and success to reach this point. I am glad that I was able to share it with you.

As you close this book, I invite you to remember your accomplishments and determination. Reading this book will put you in the right direction to grow.

Keep up the good work and do not forget that HR can be sexy when you care about people.

www.ingramcontent.com/pod-product-compliance
Lightning Source LLC
Chambersburg PA
CBHW070617220526
45466CB00001B/35